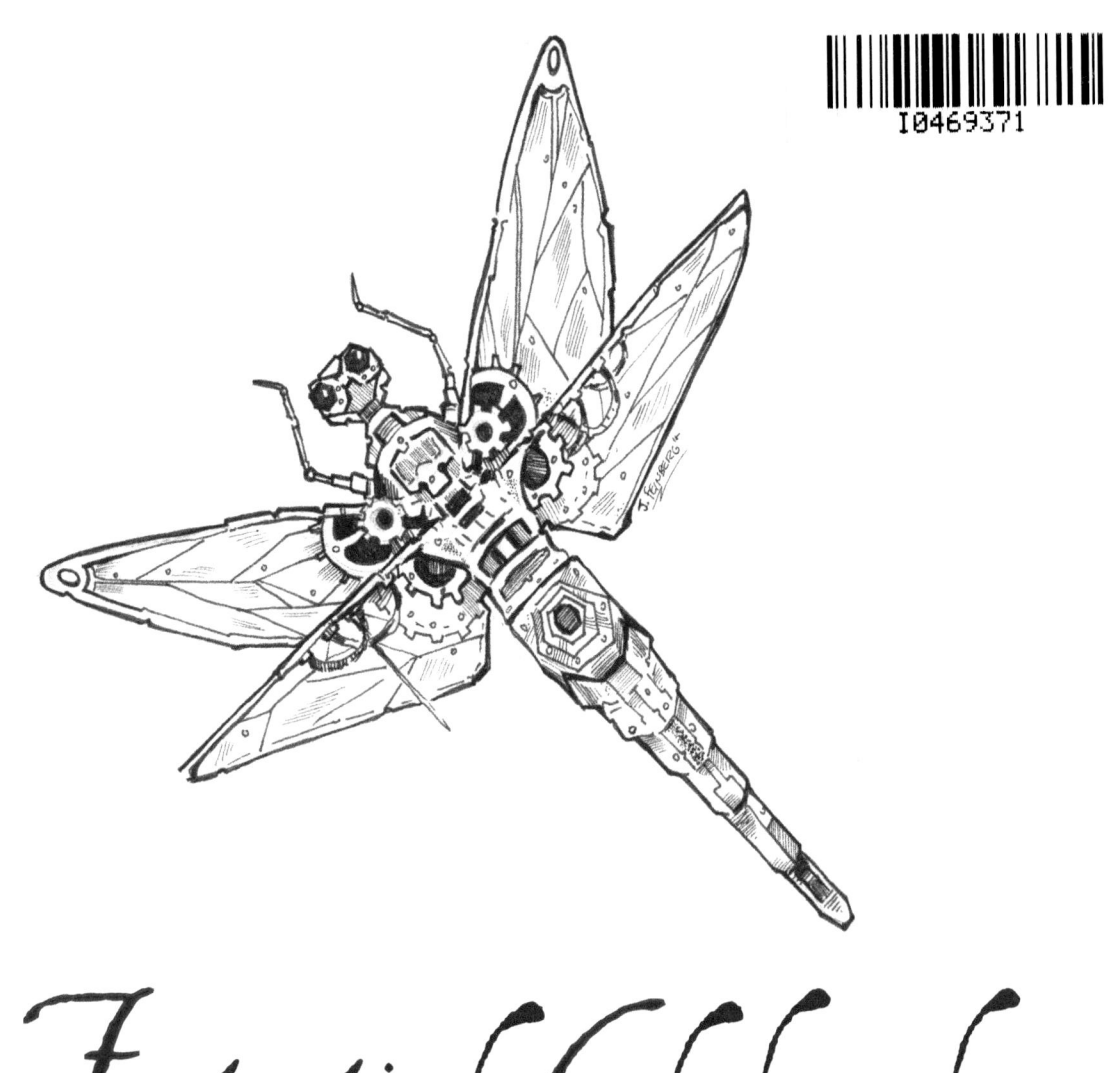

Fantastical Clockwork

COLORING BOOK

BY JESSICA CATHRYN FEINBERG

With special thanks to:

All the fans, friends, and Kickstarter backers
whose support made this book possible!

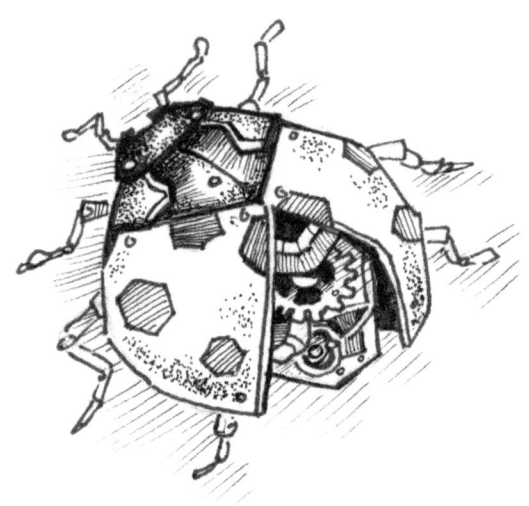

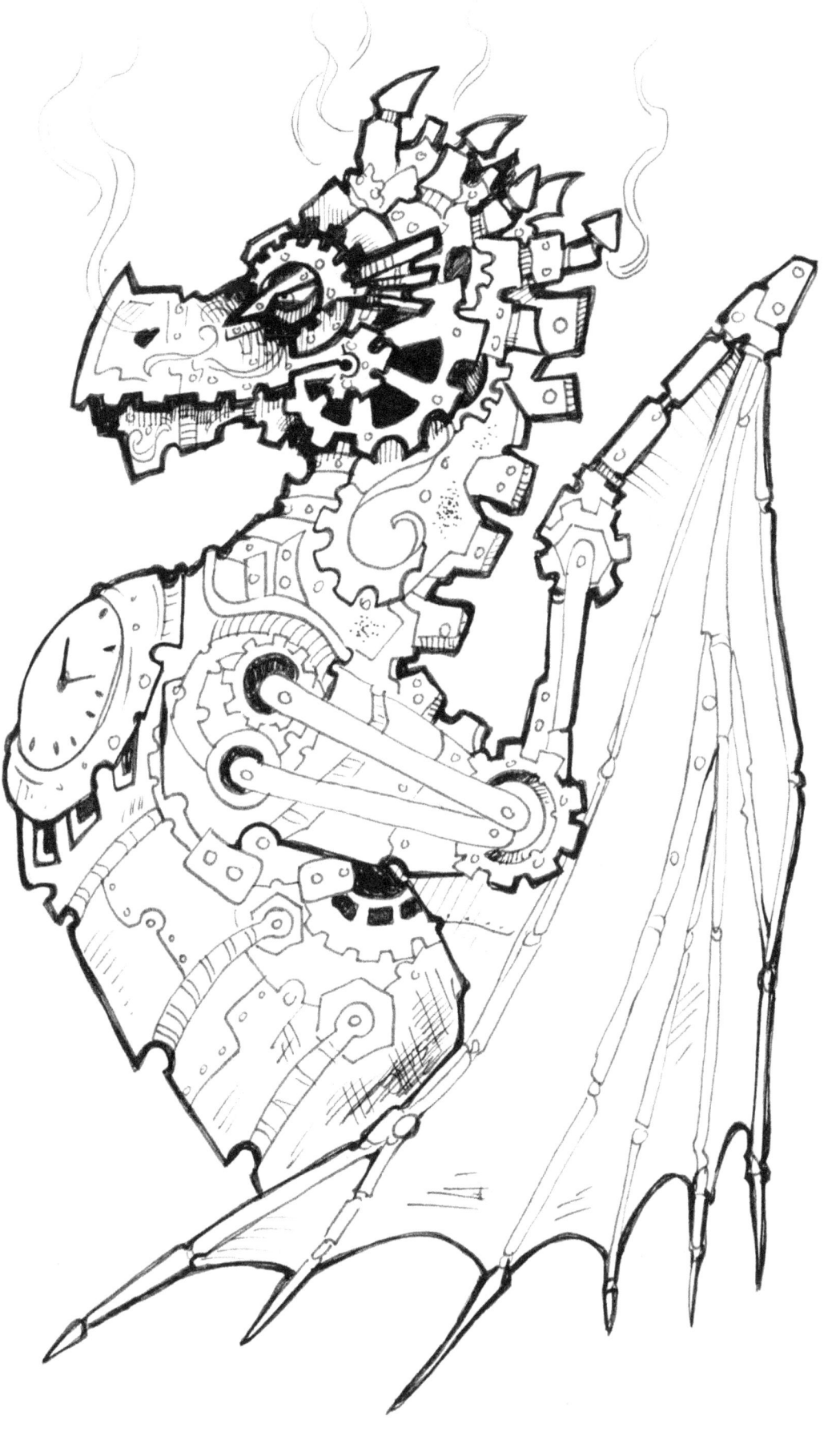

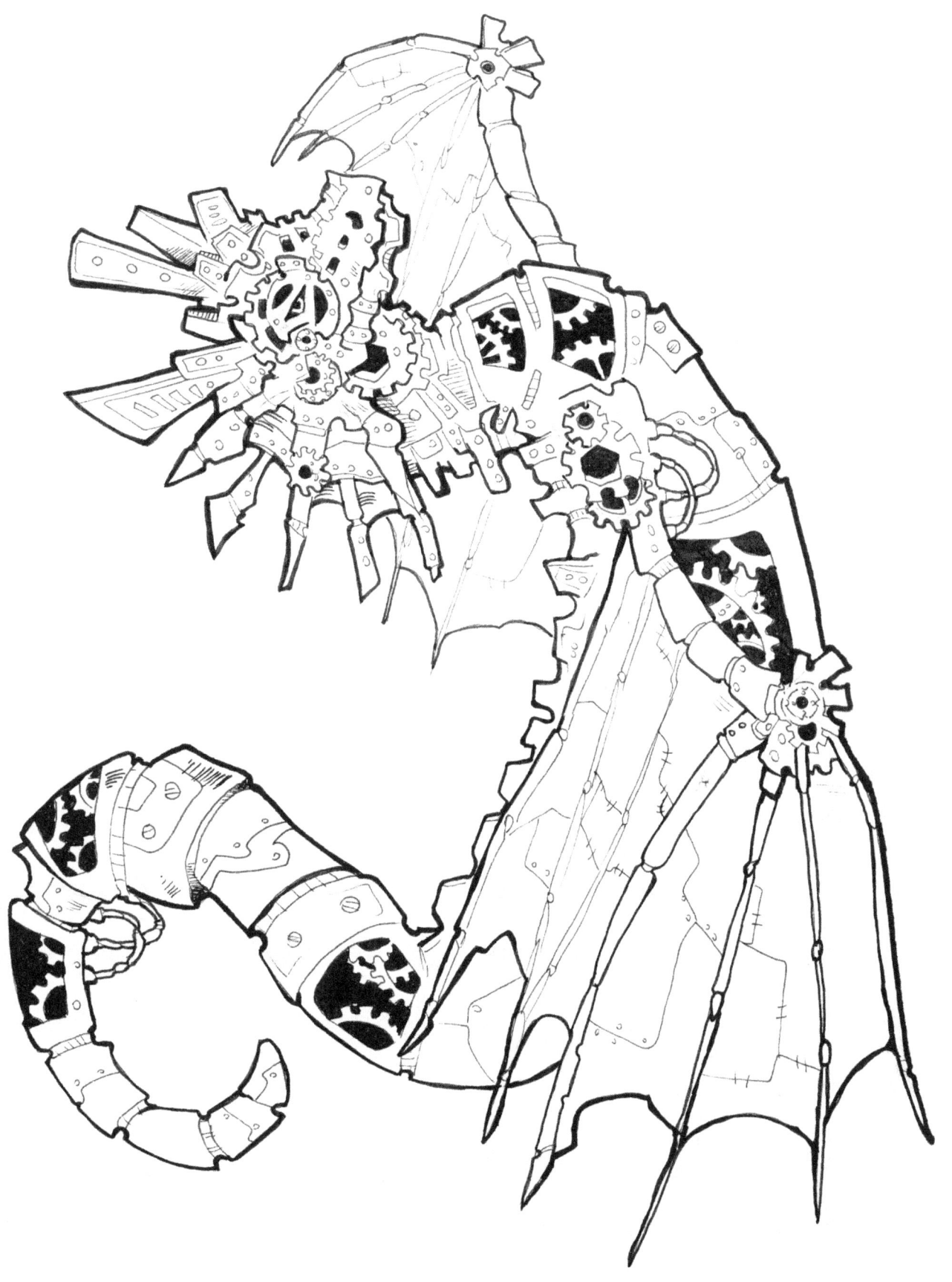

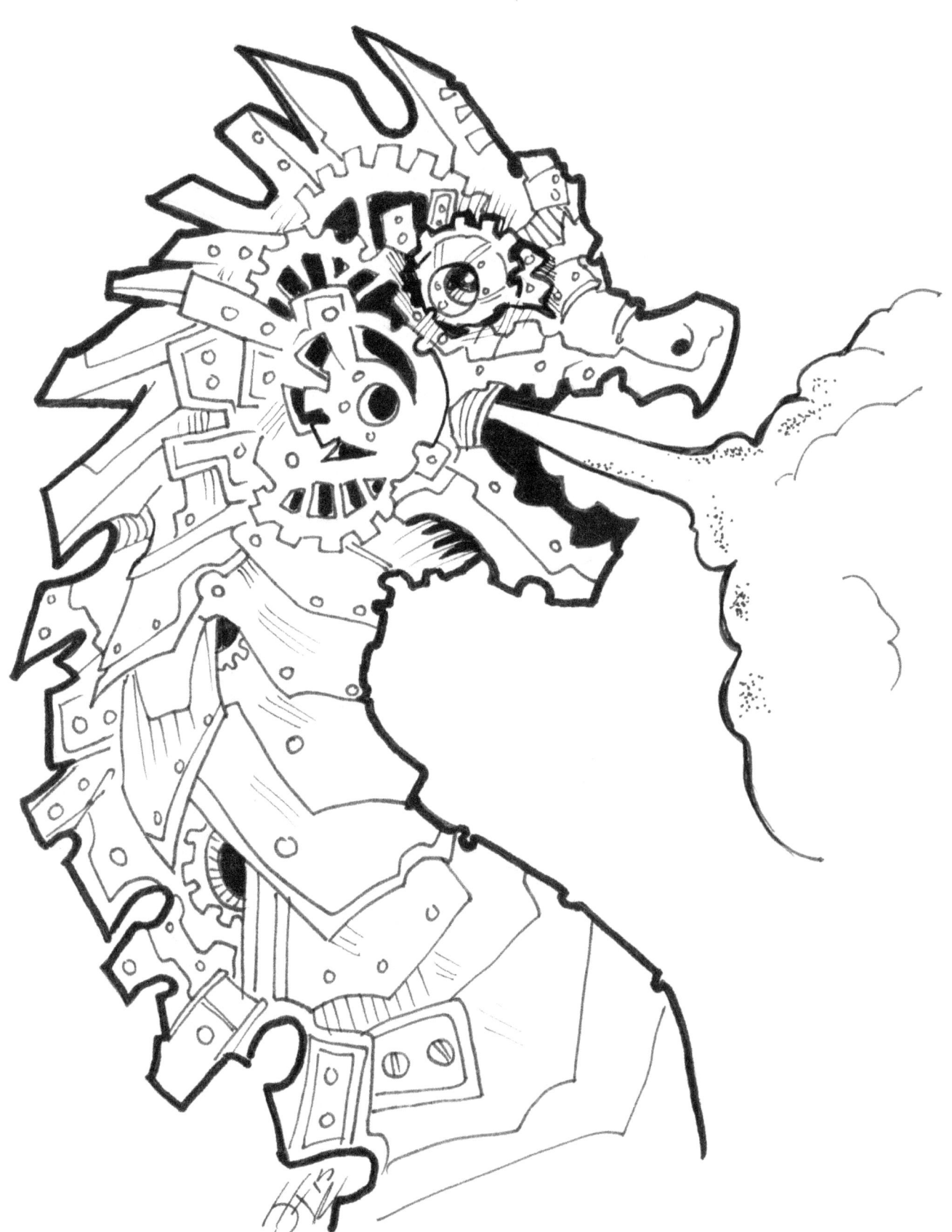

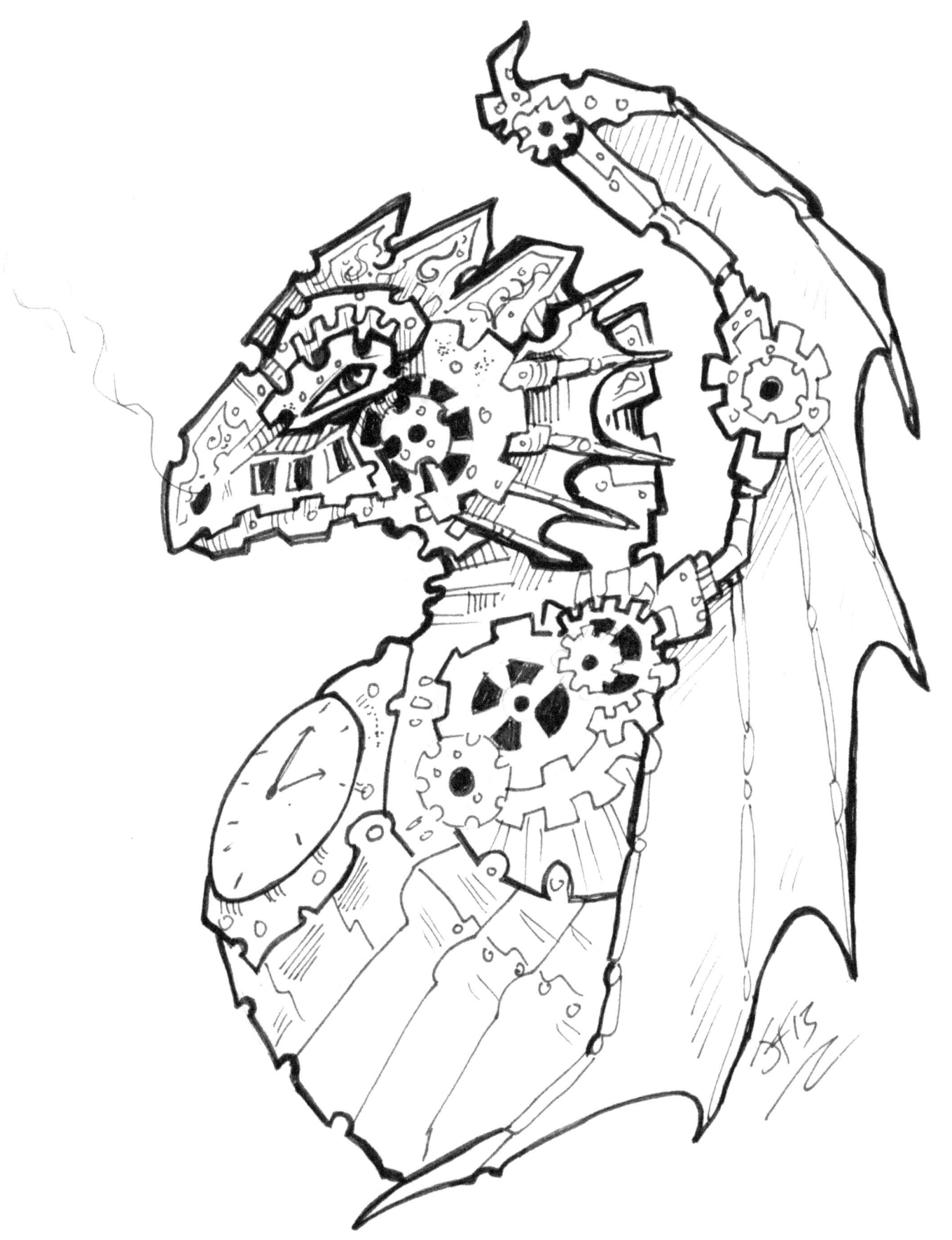

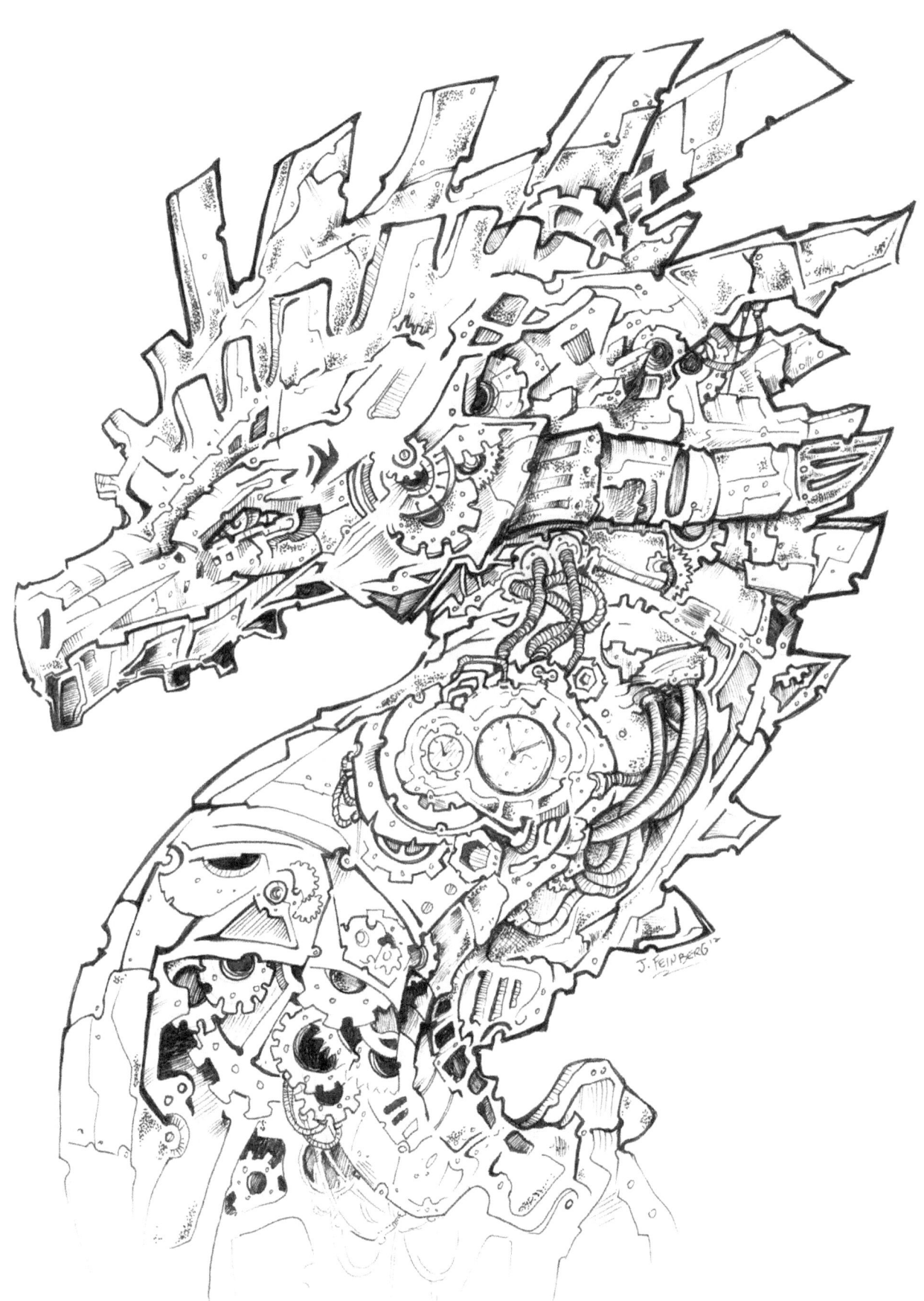

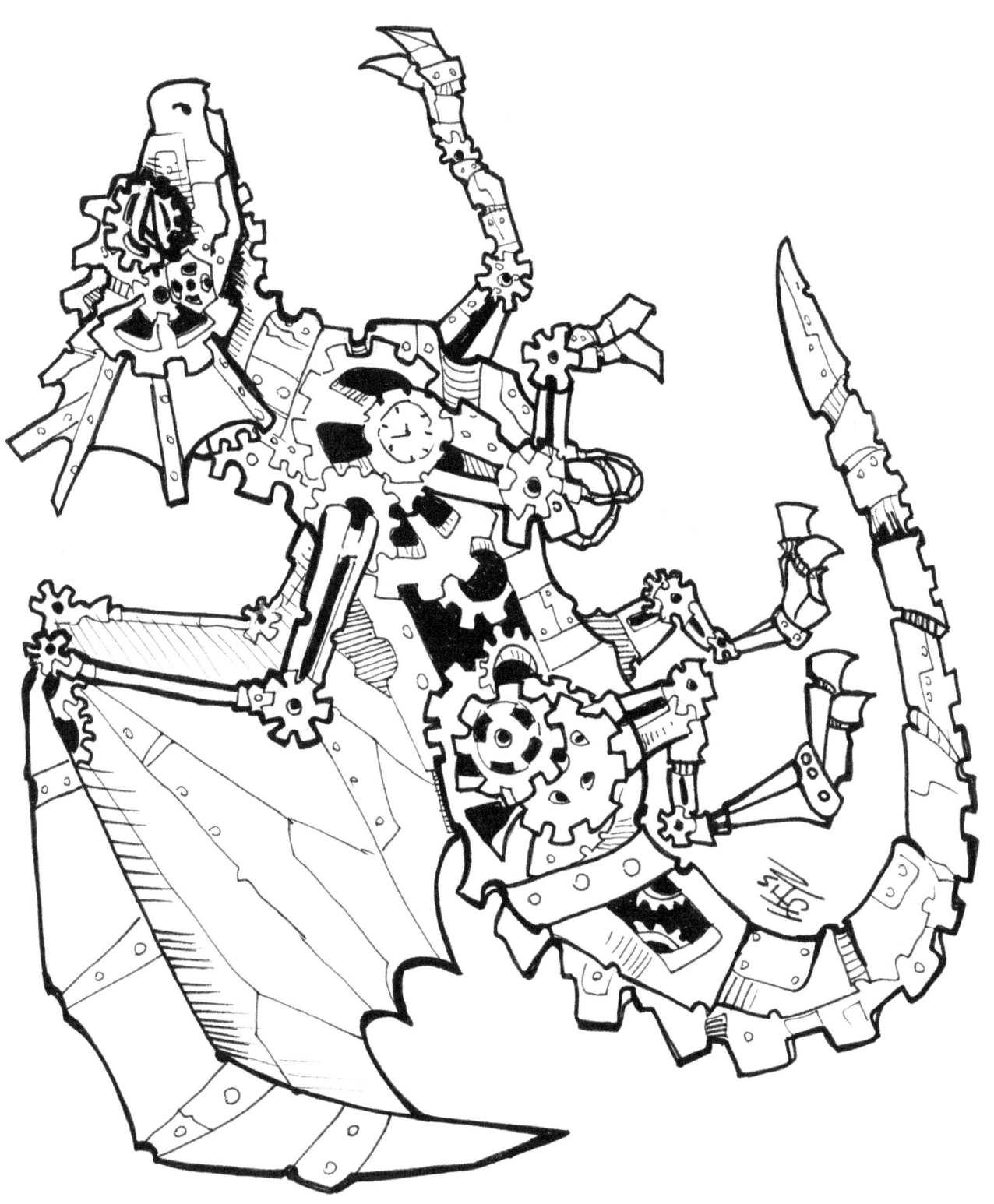

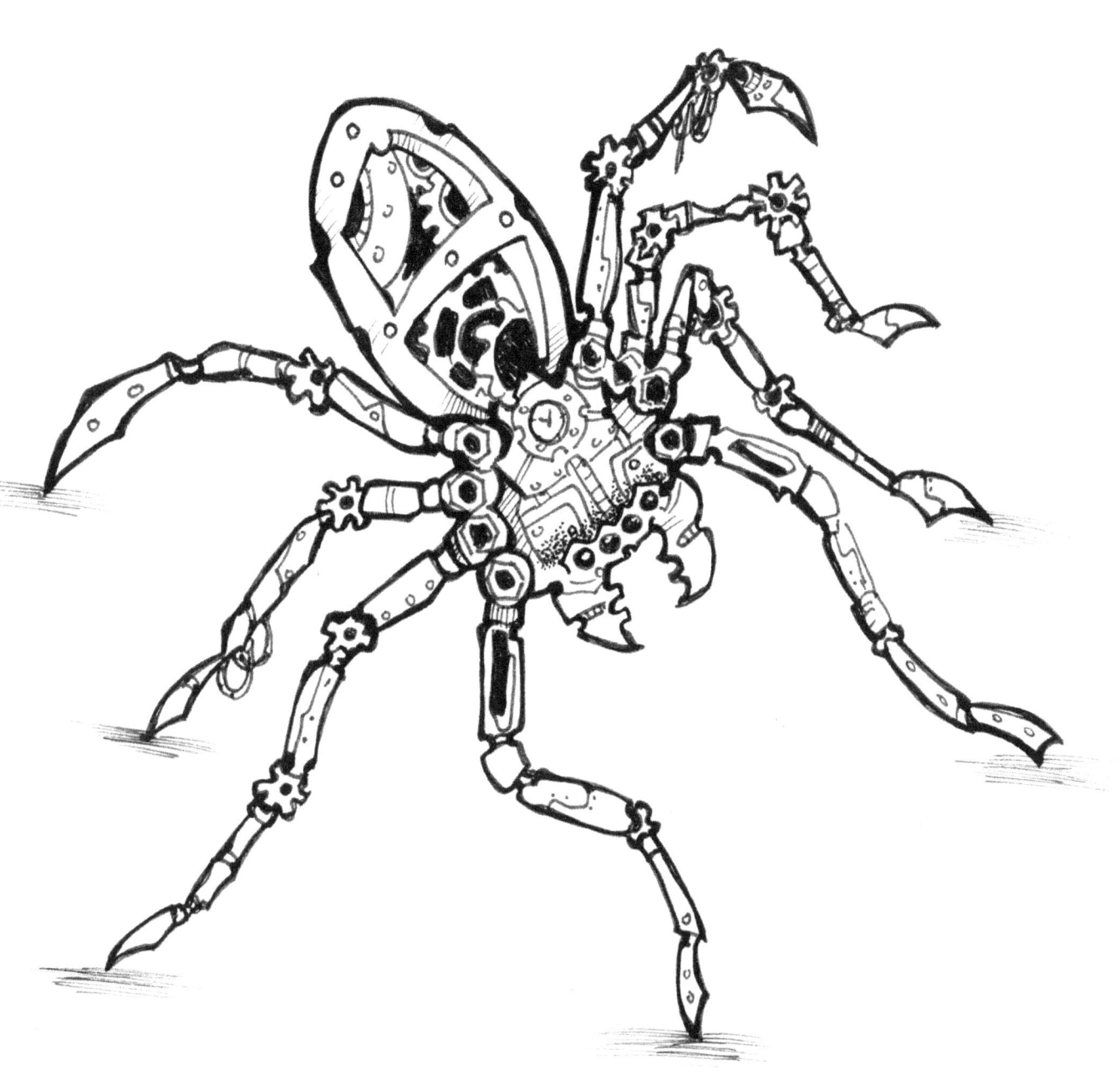

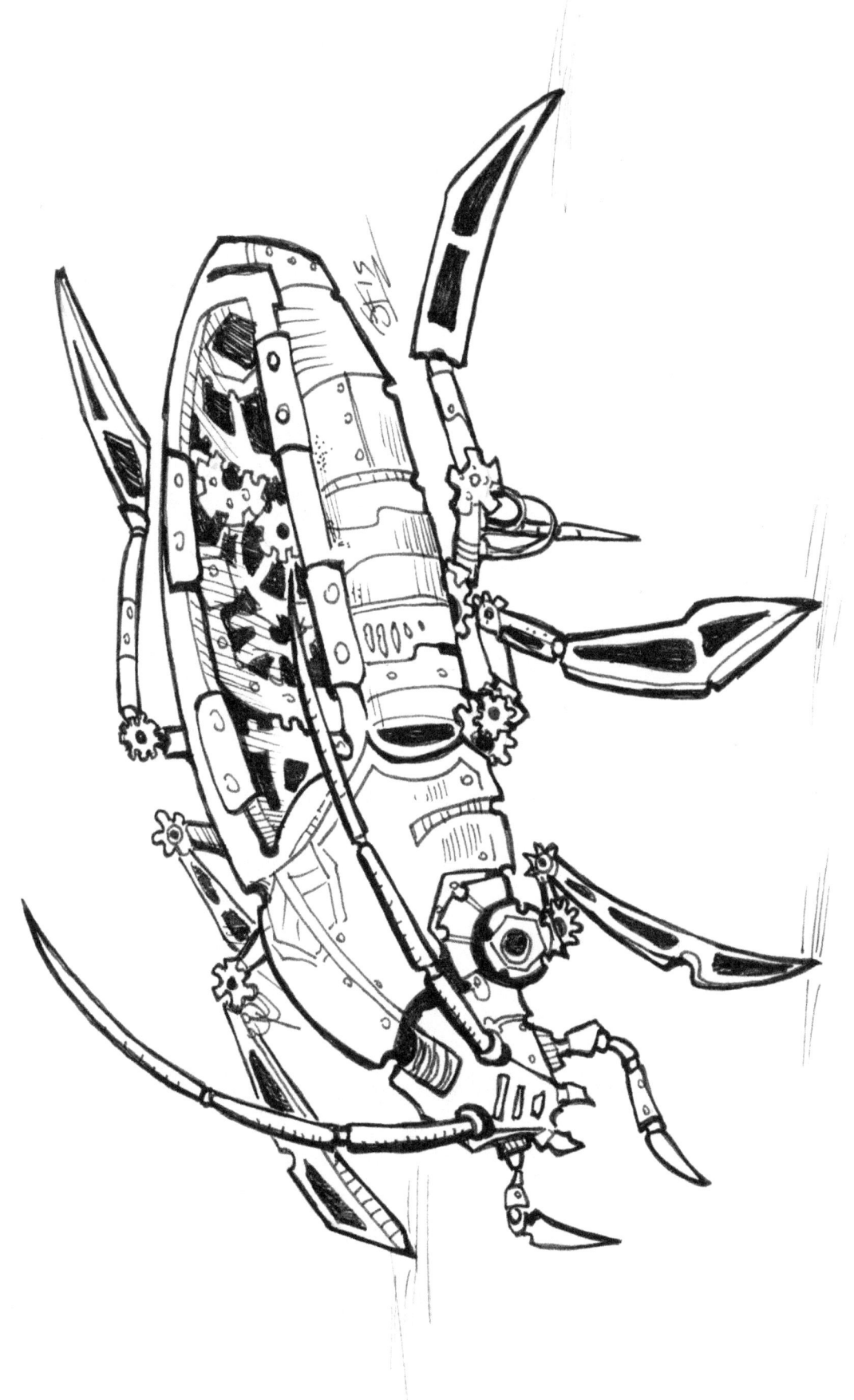

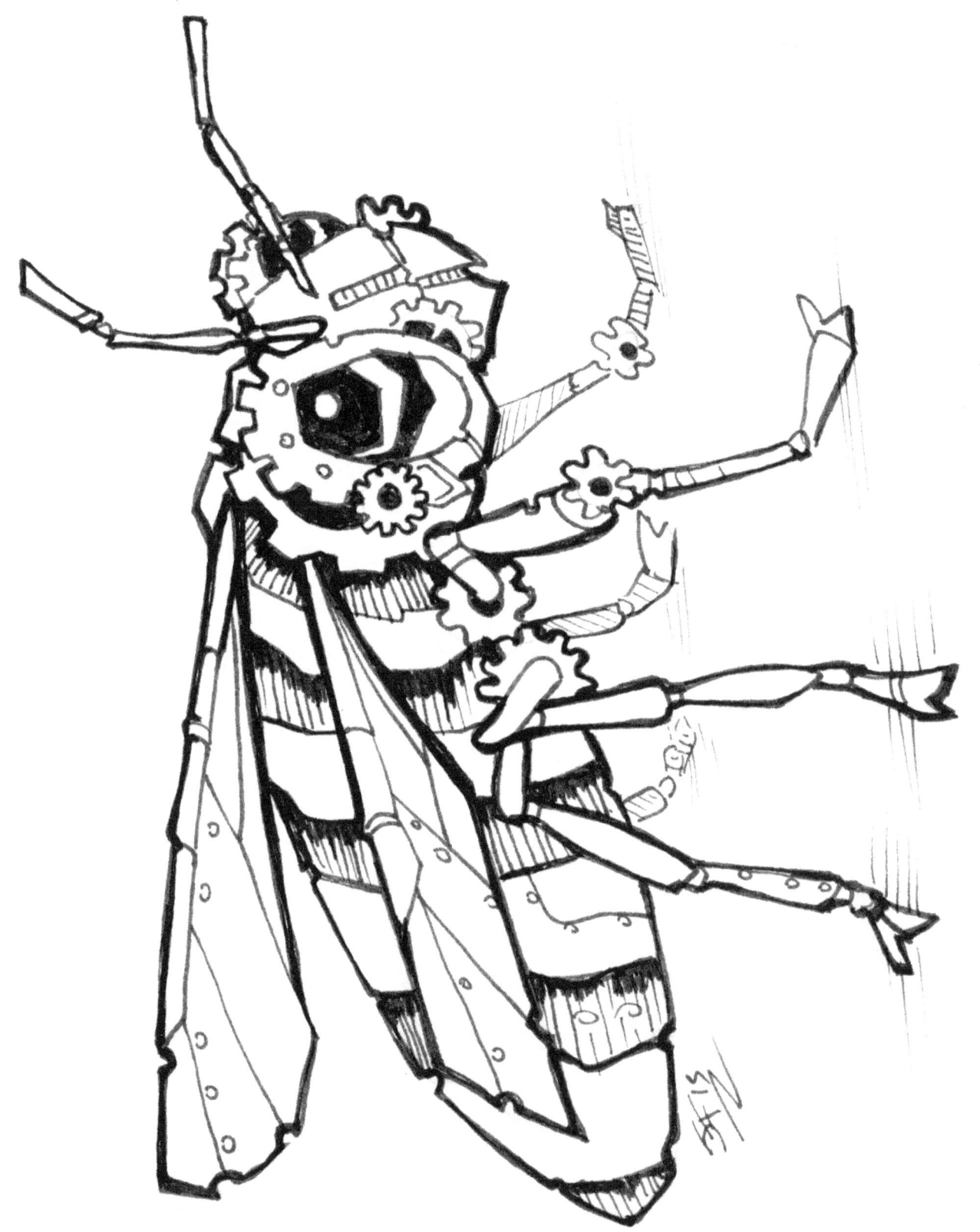

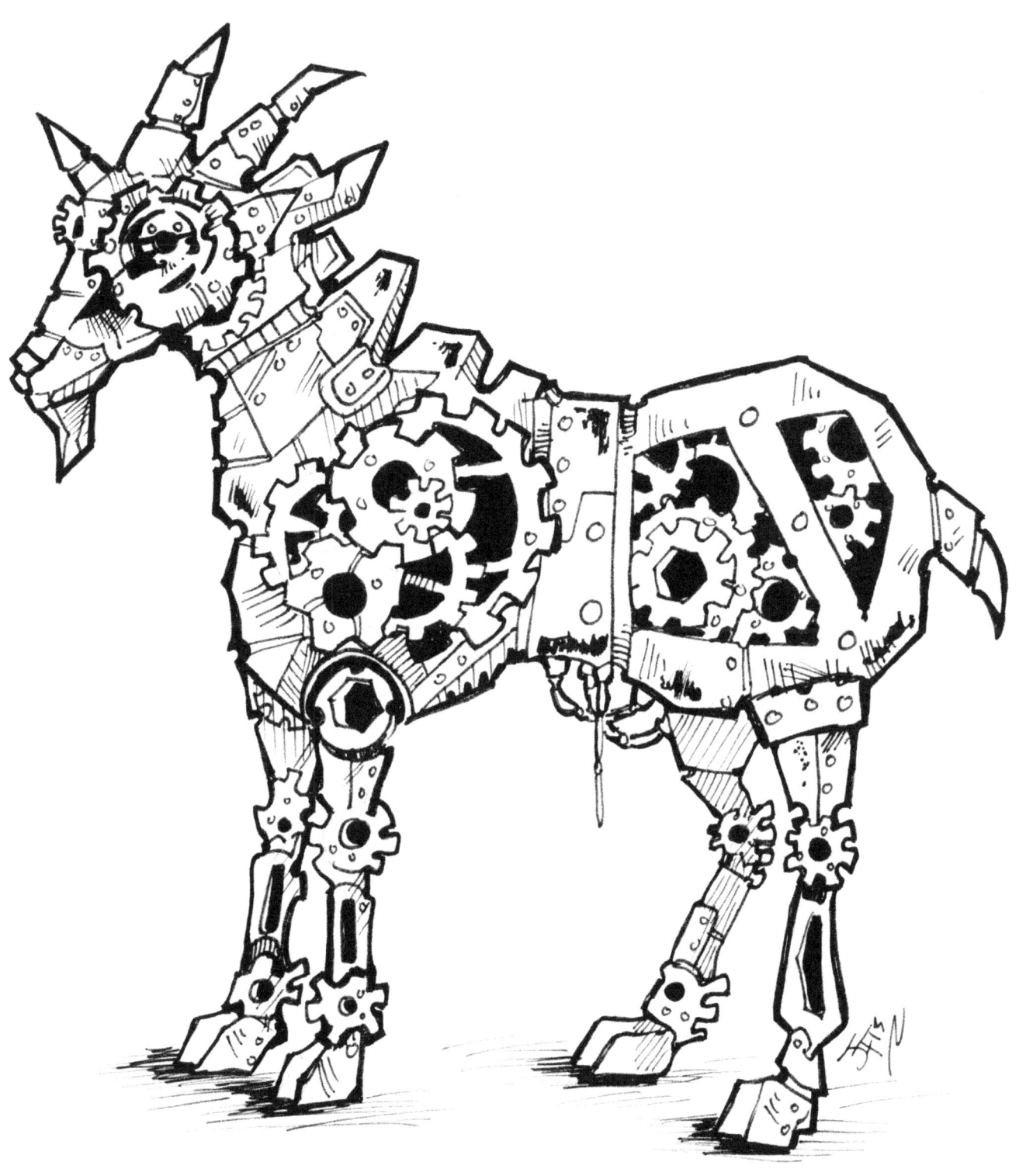

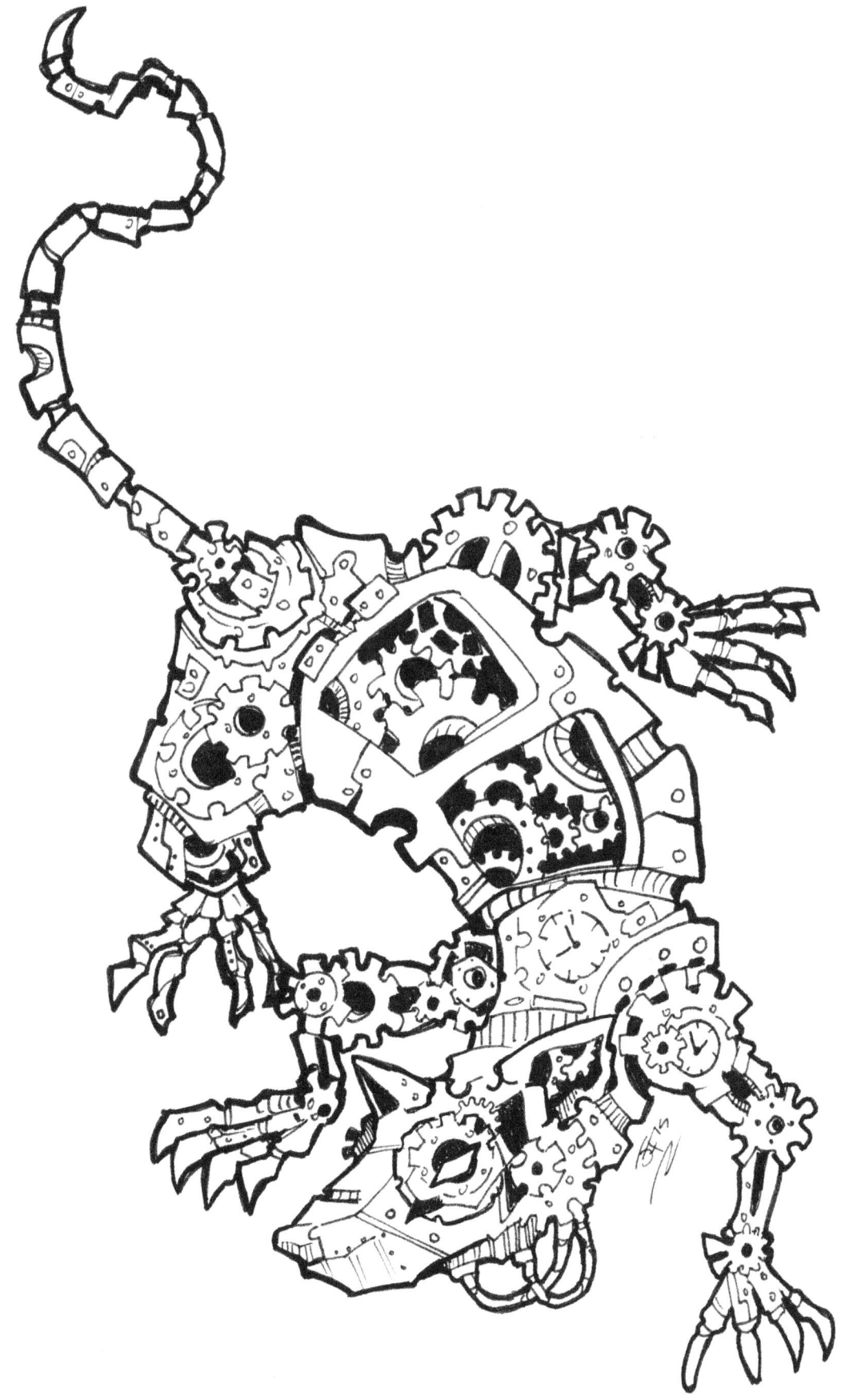

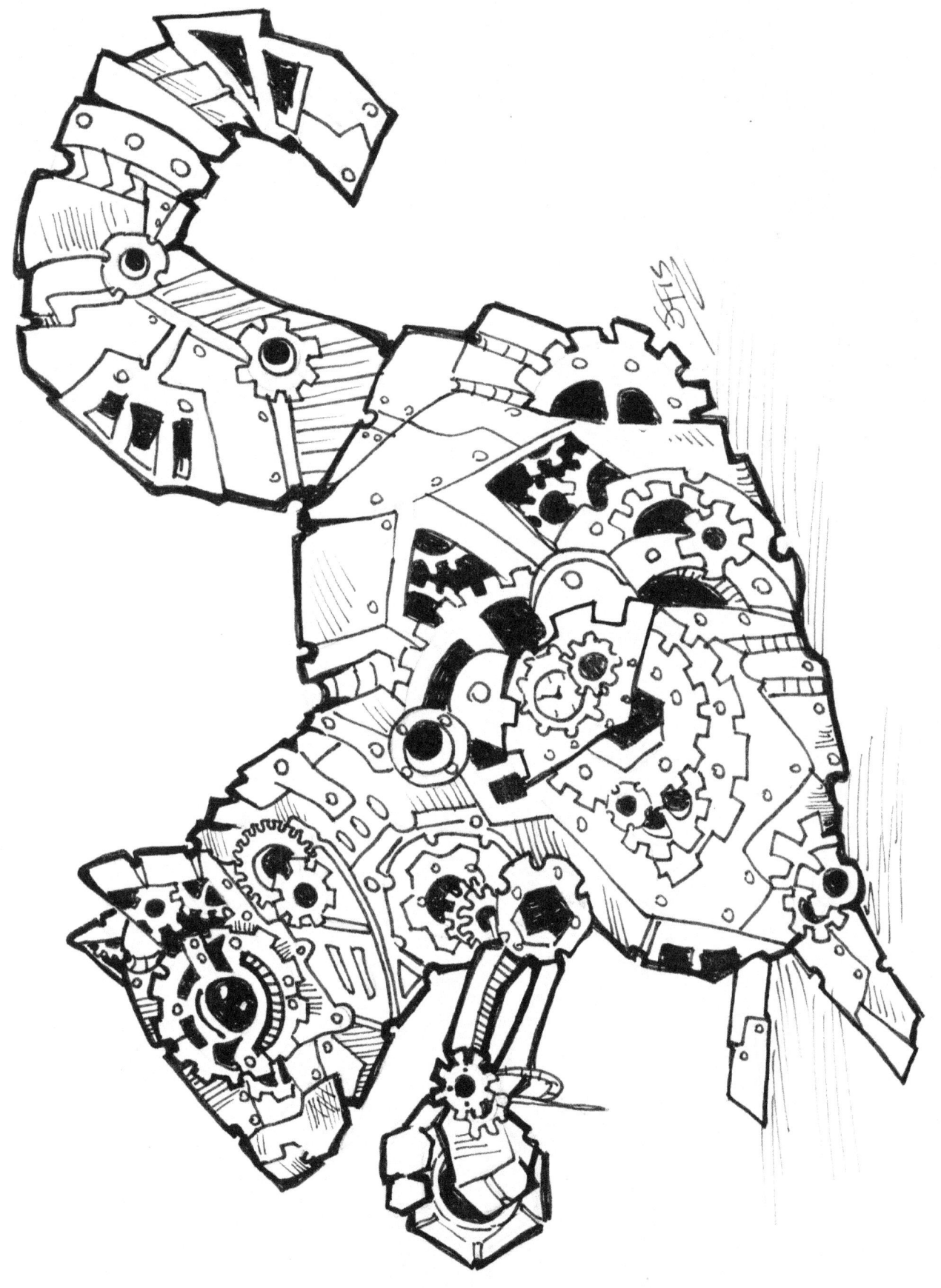

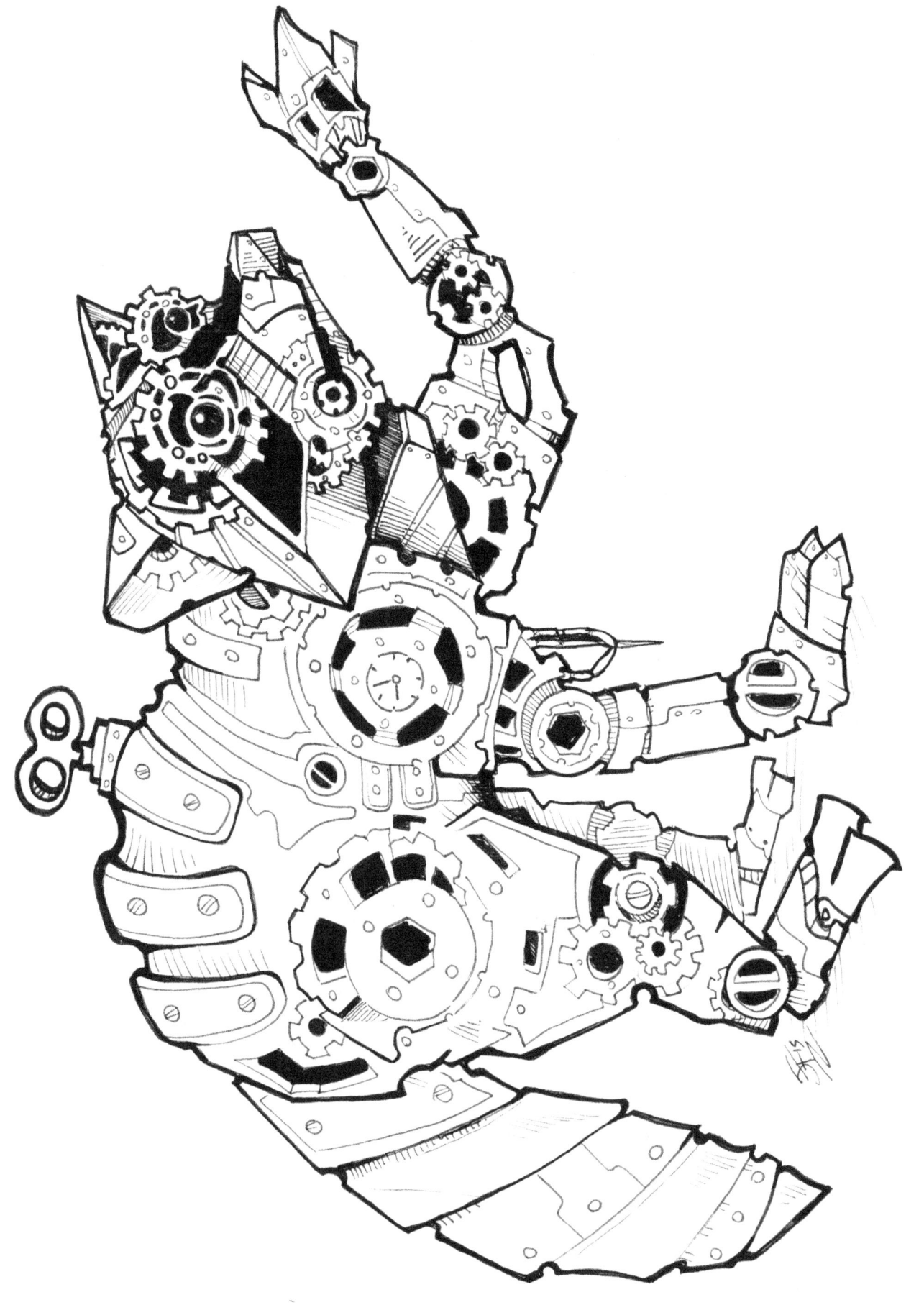

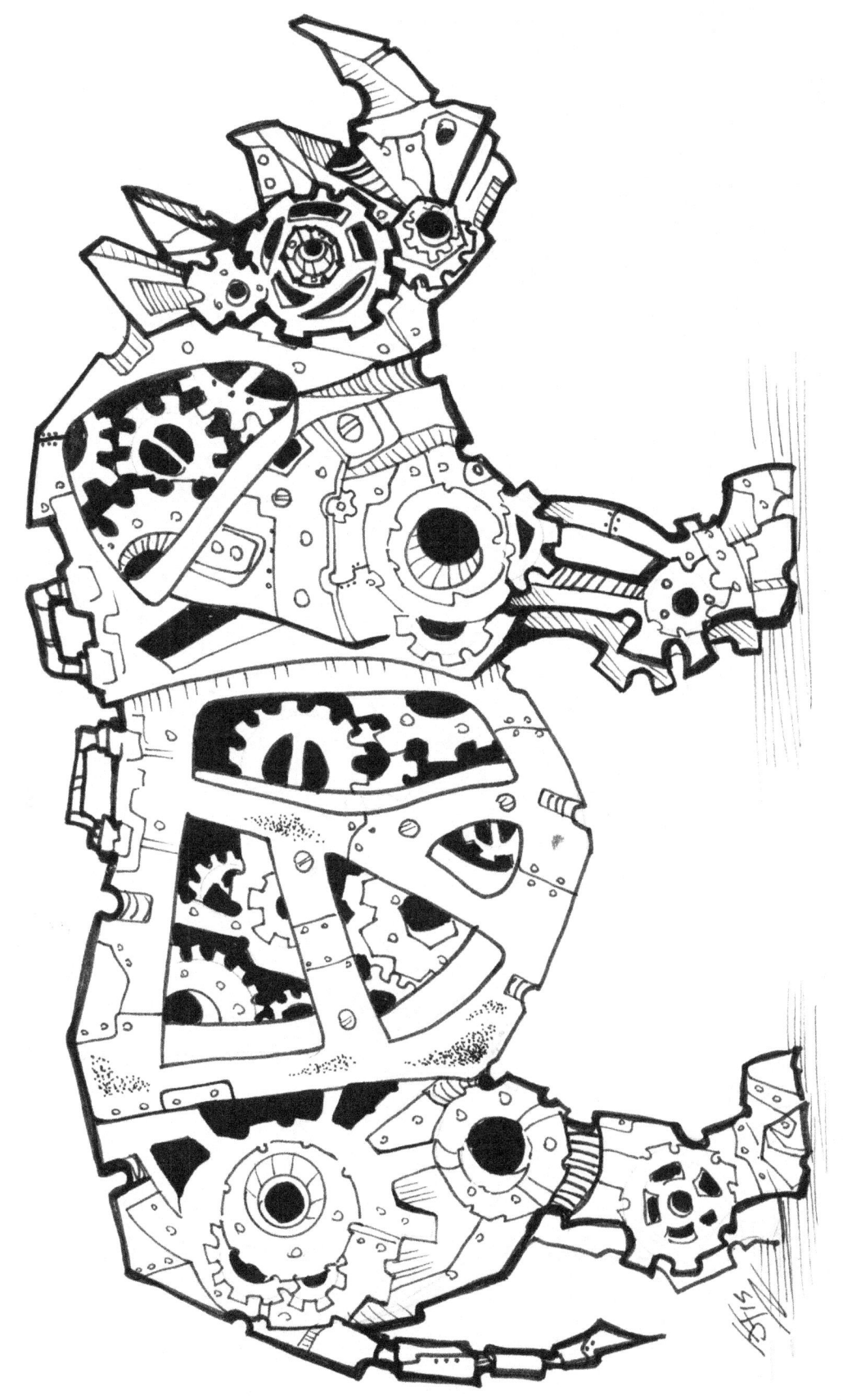

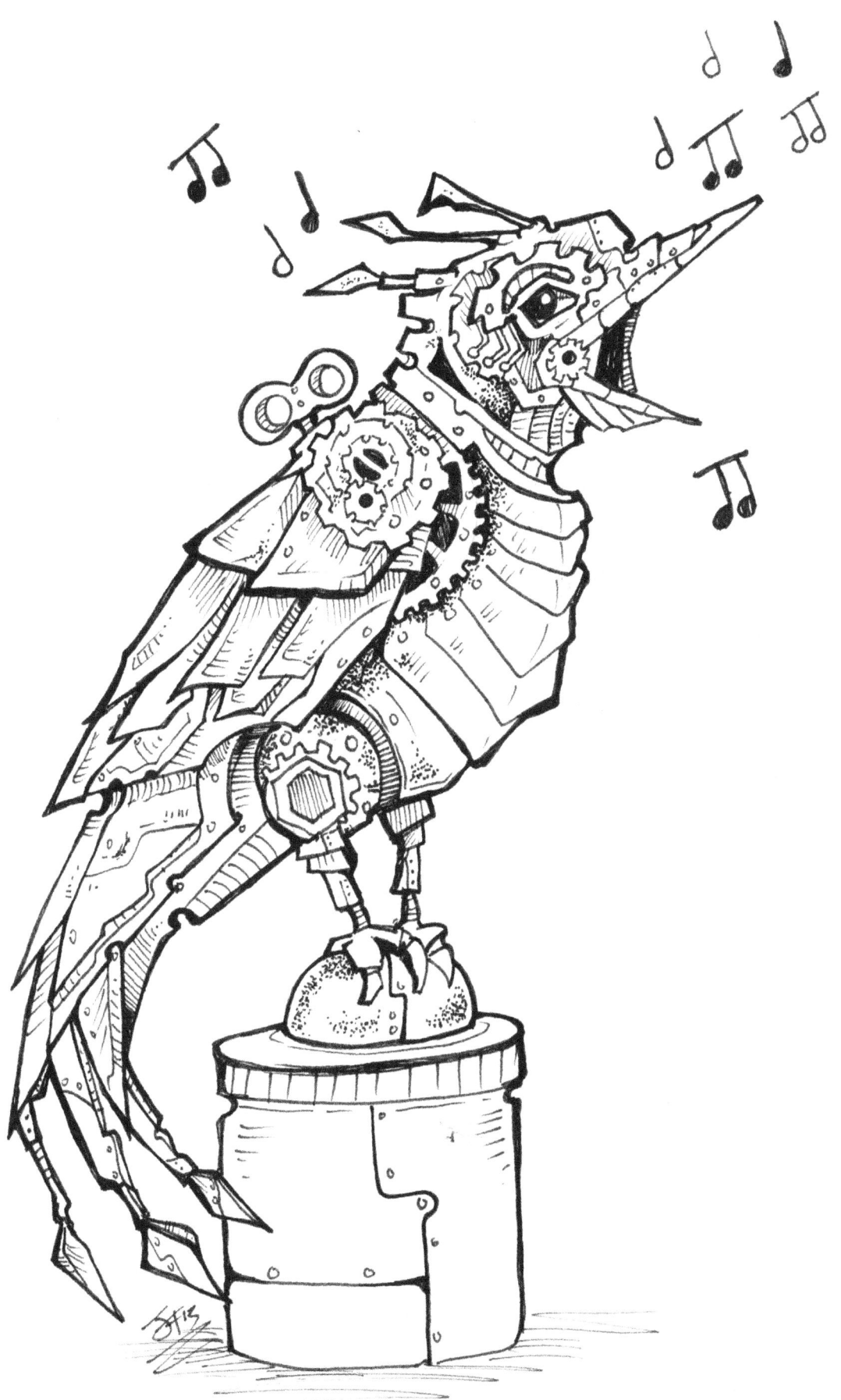

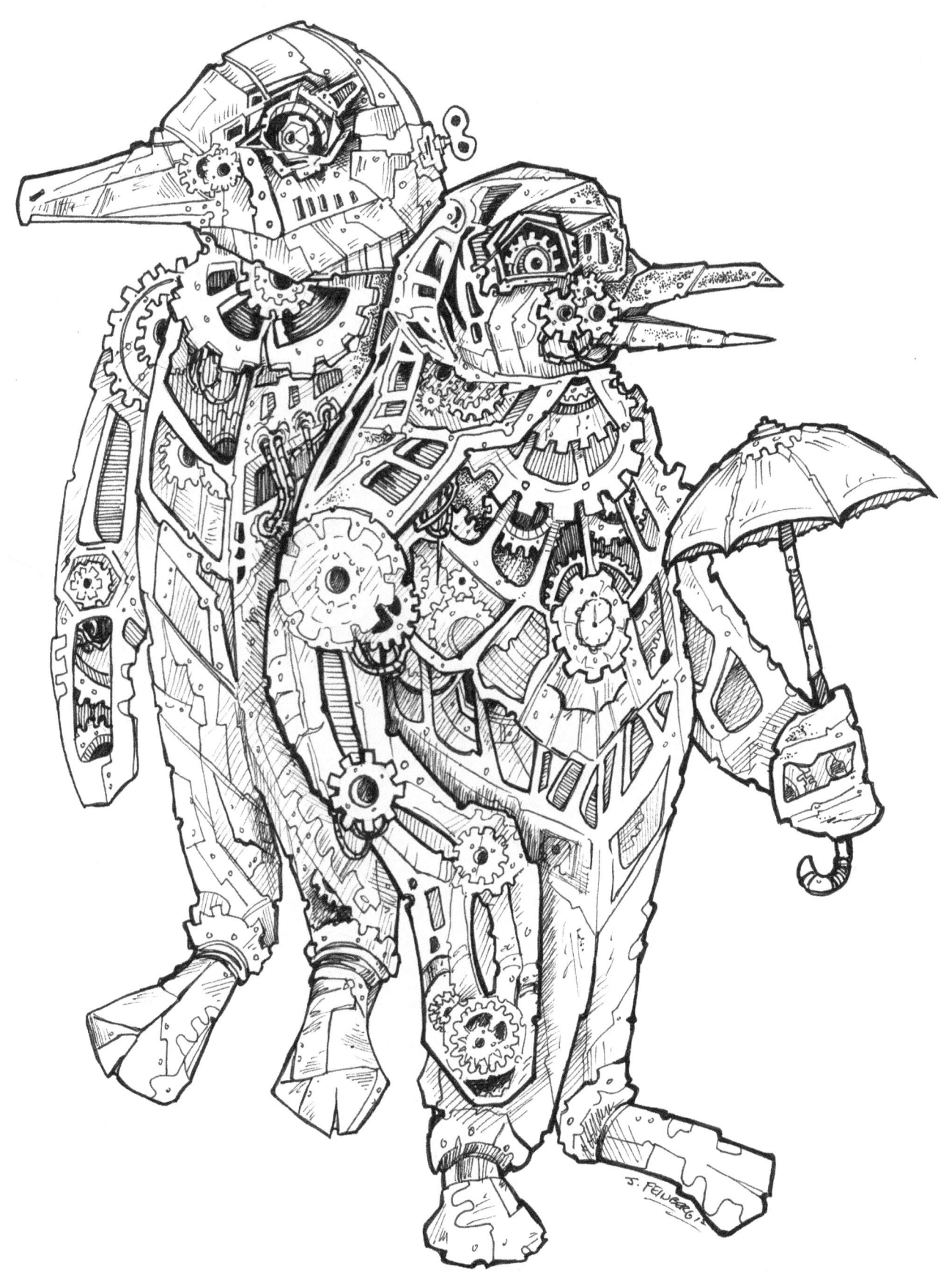

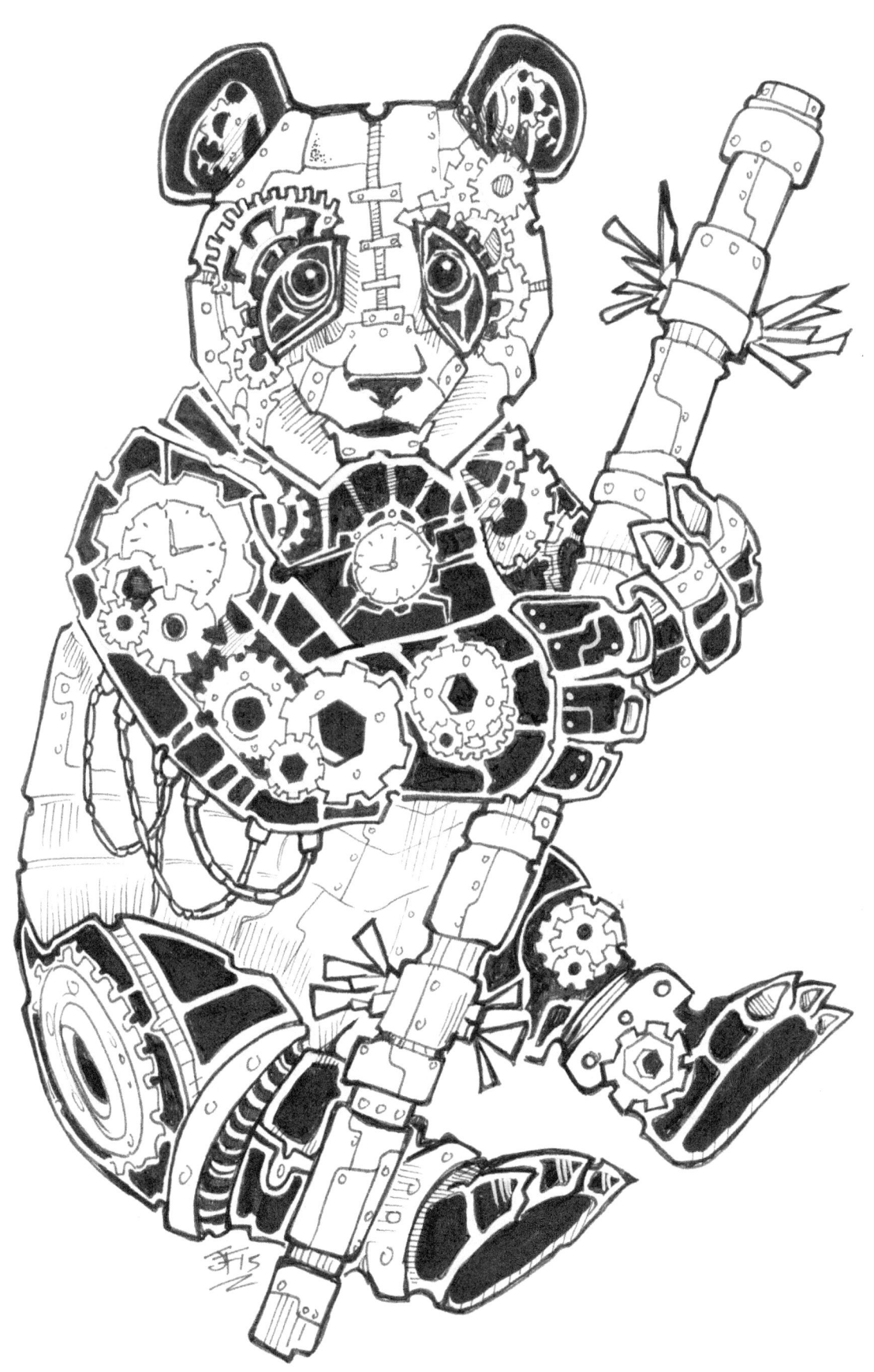

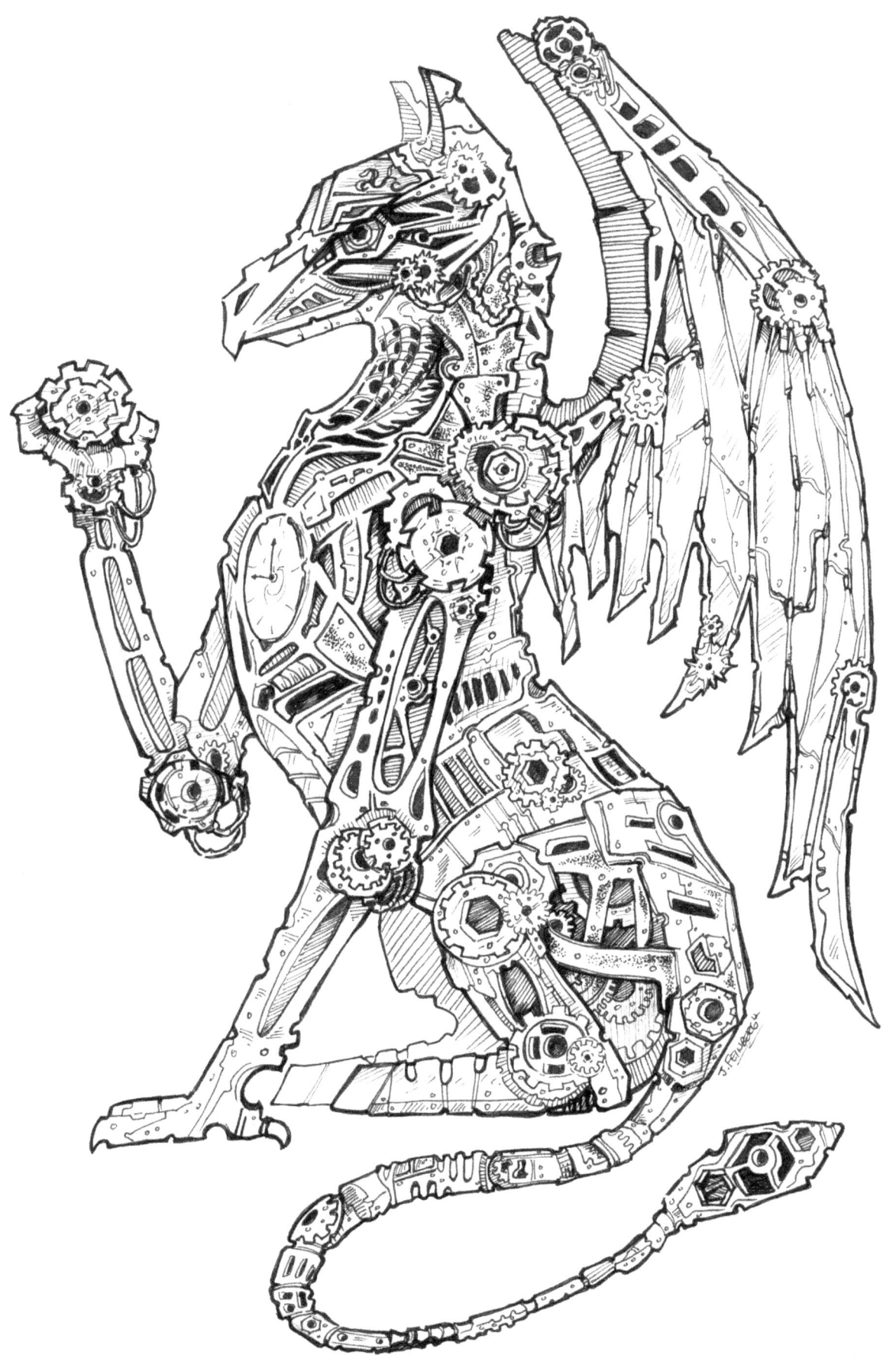

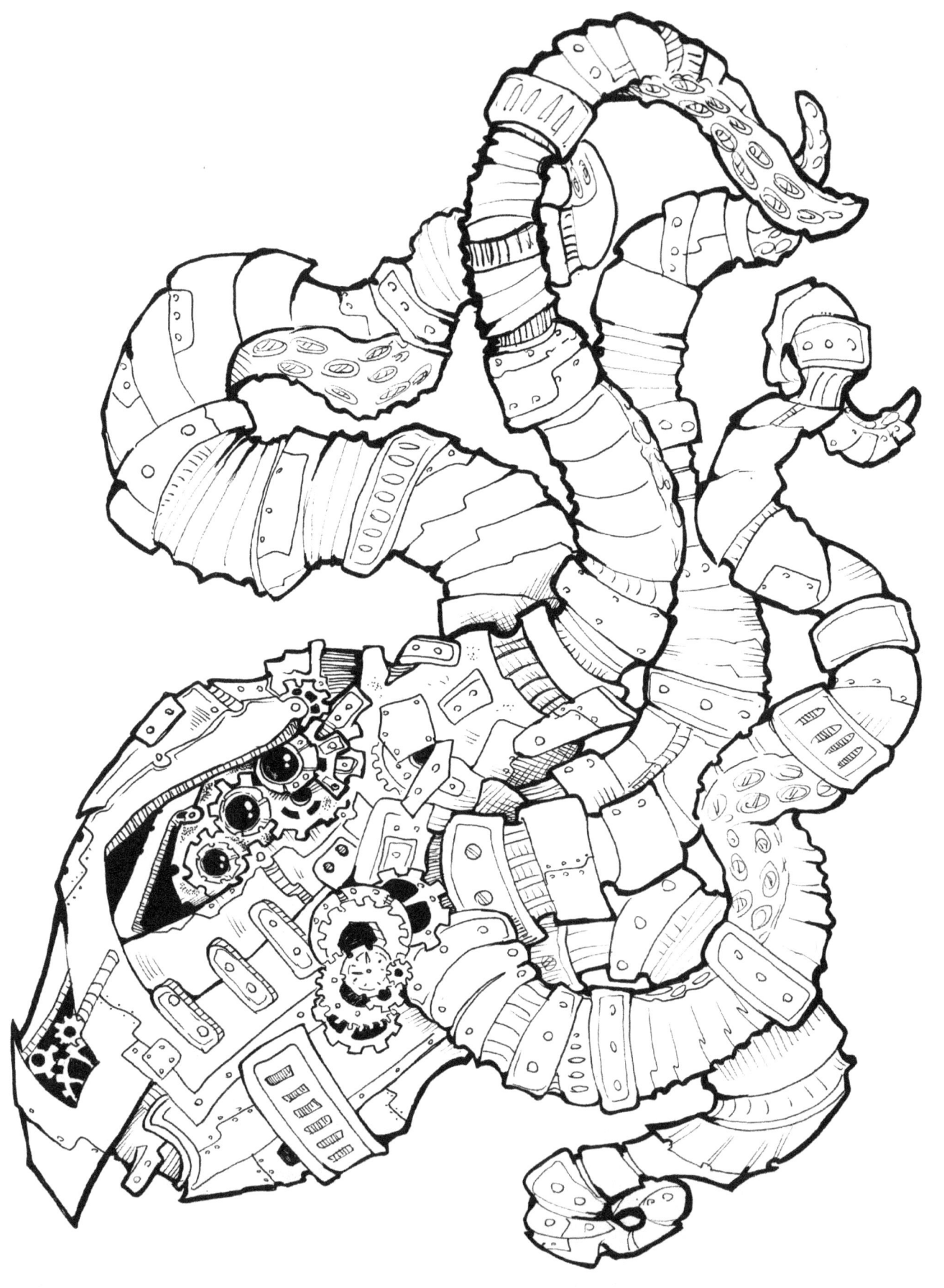

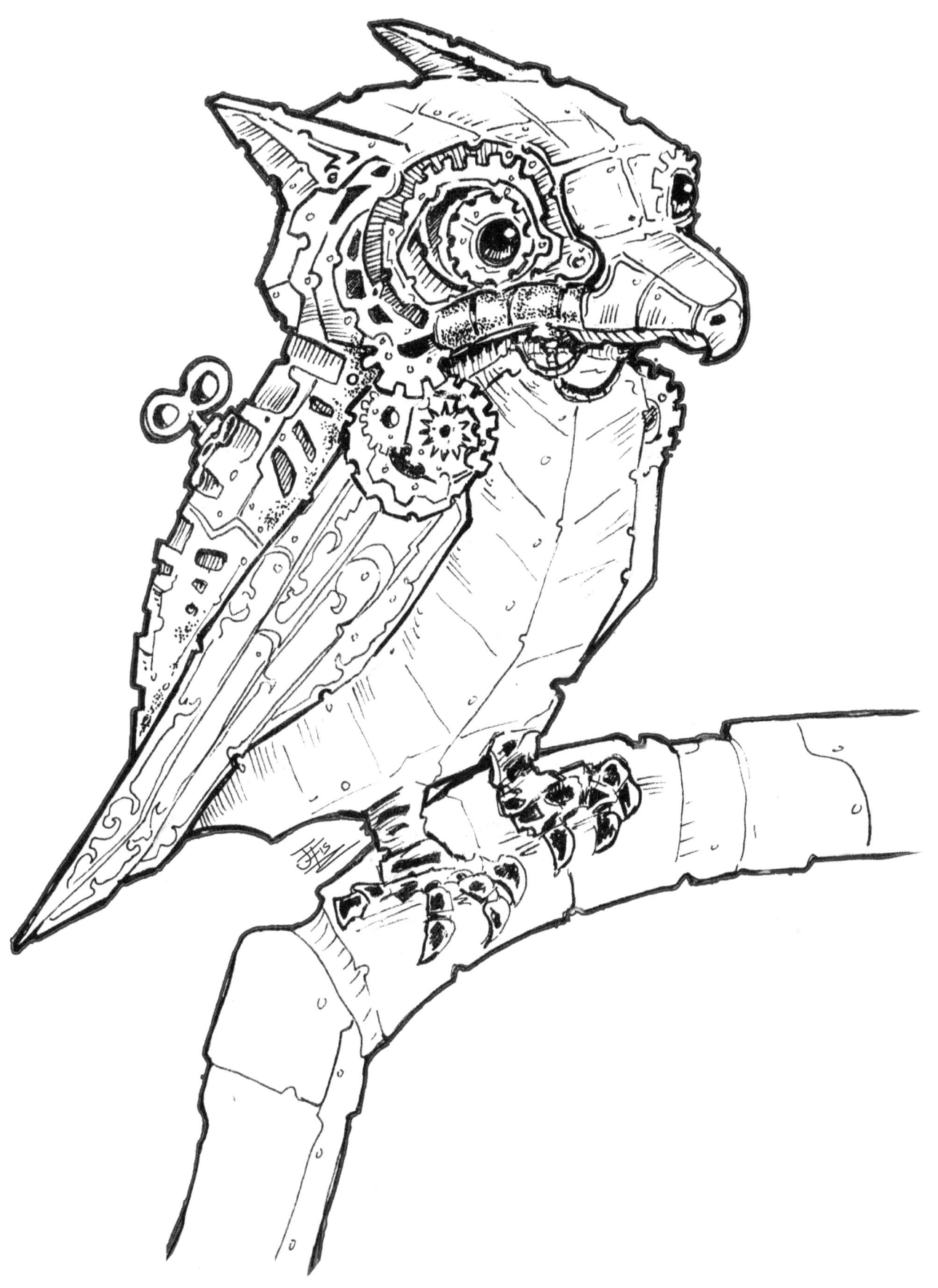

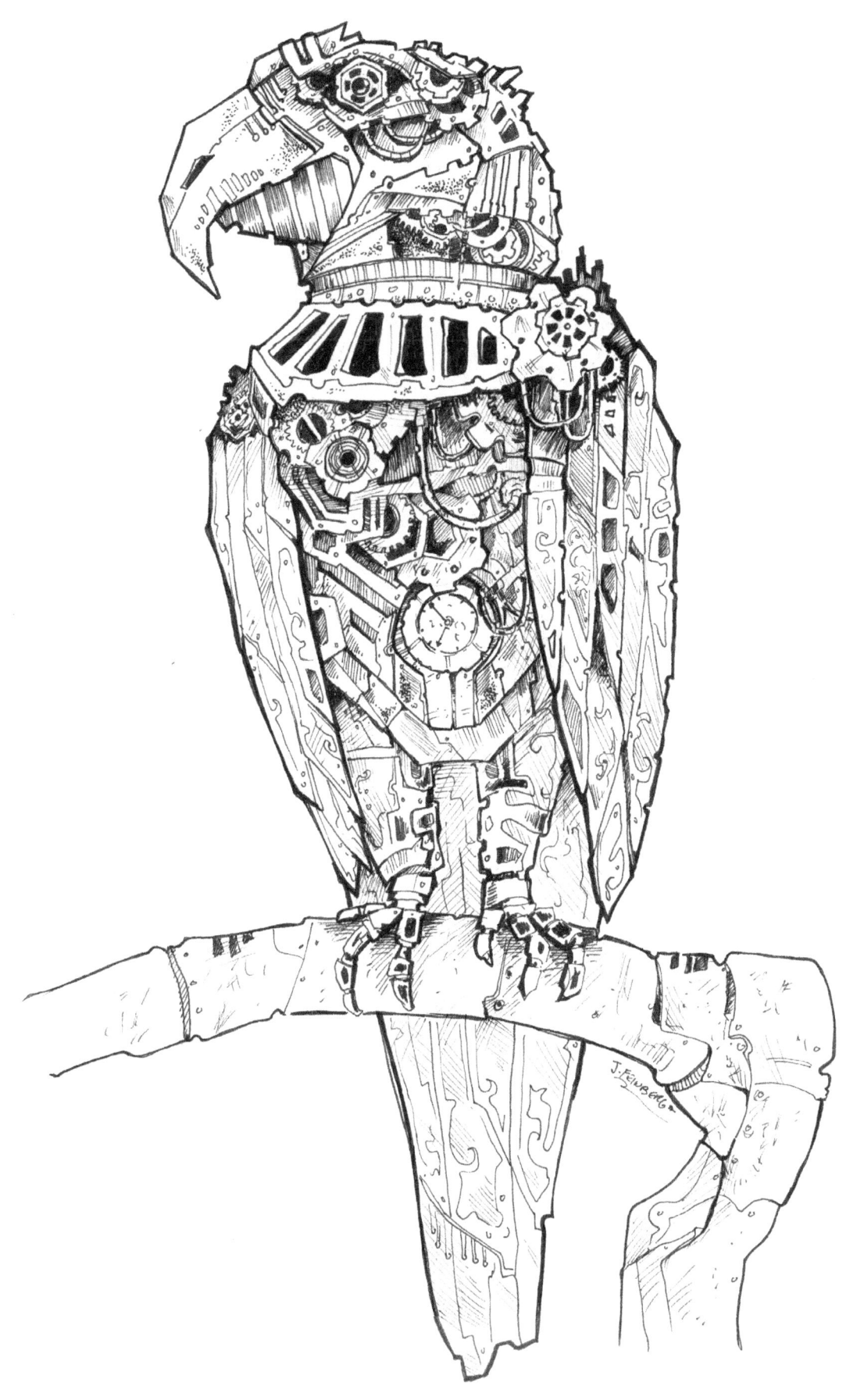

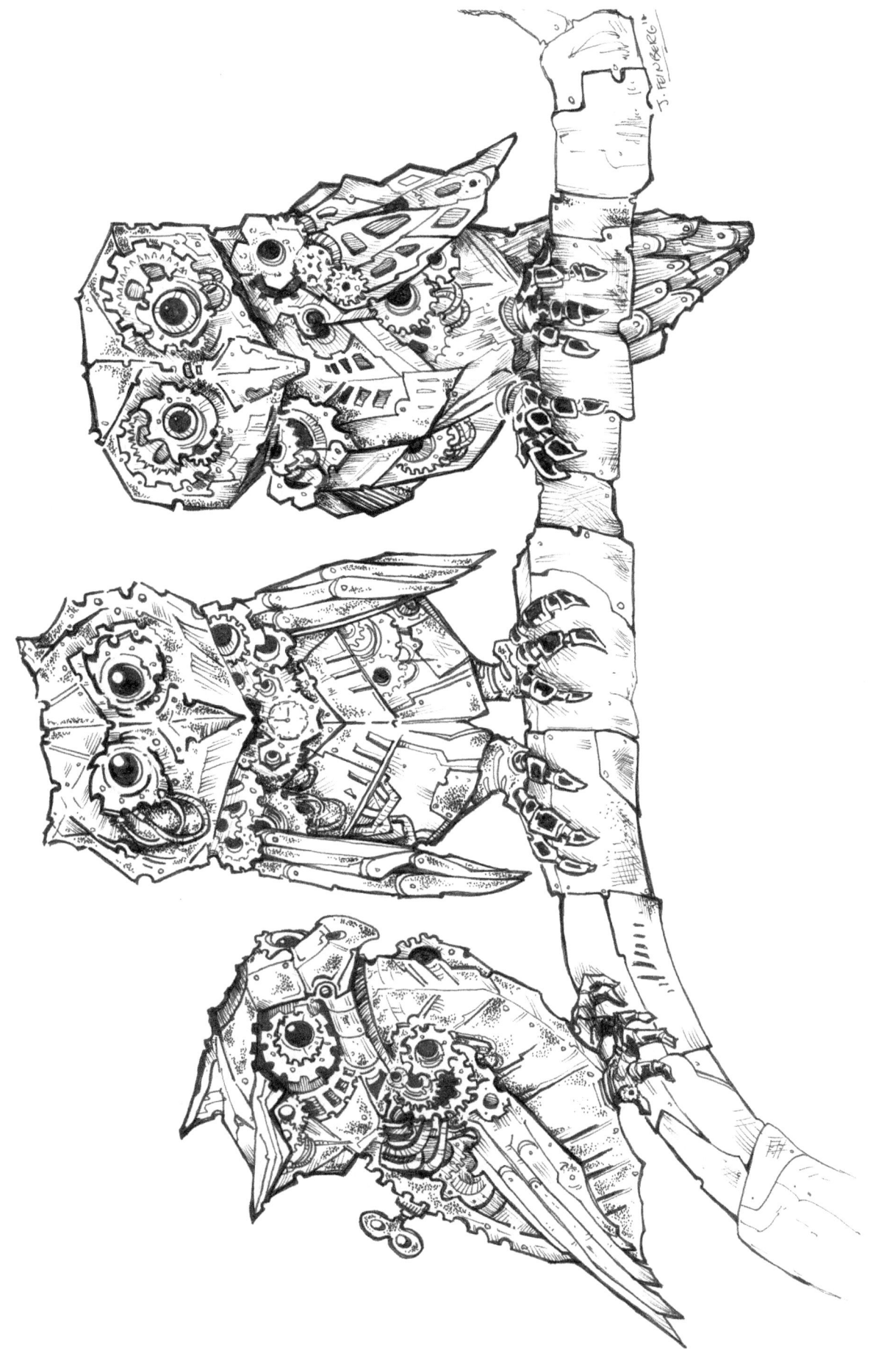

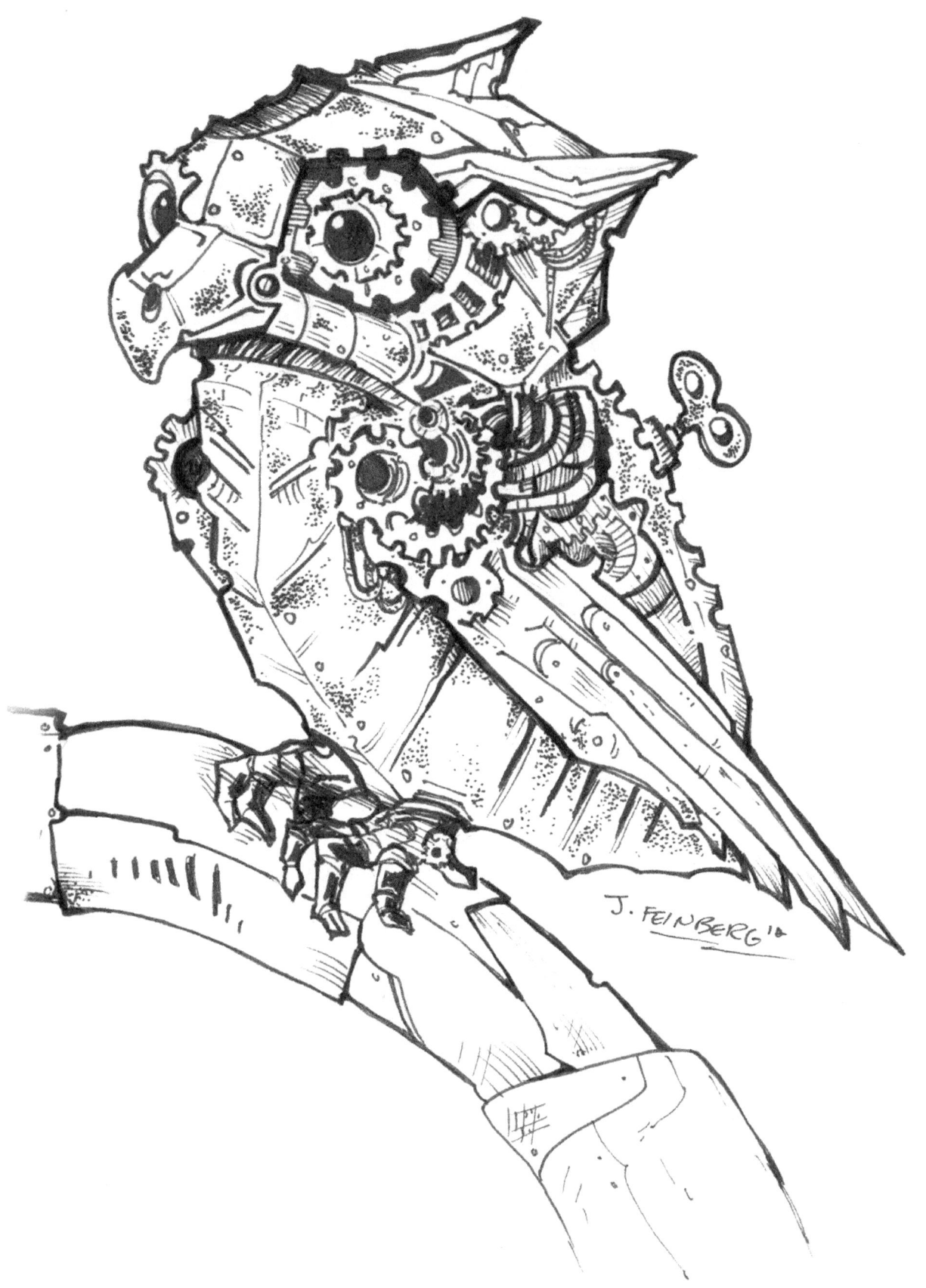

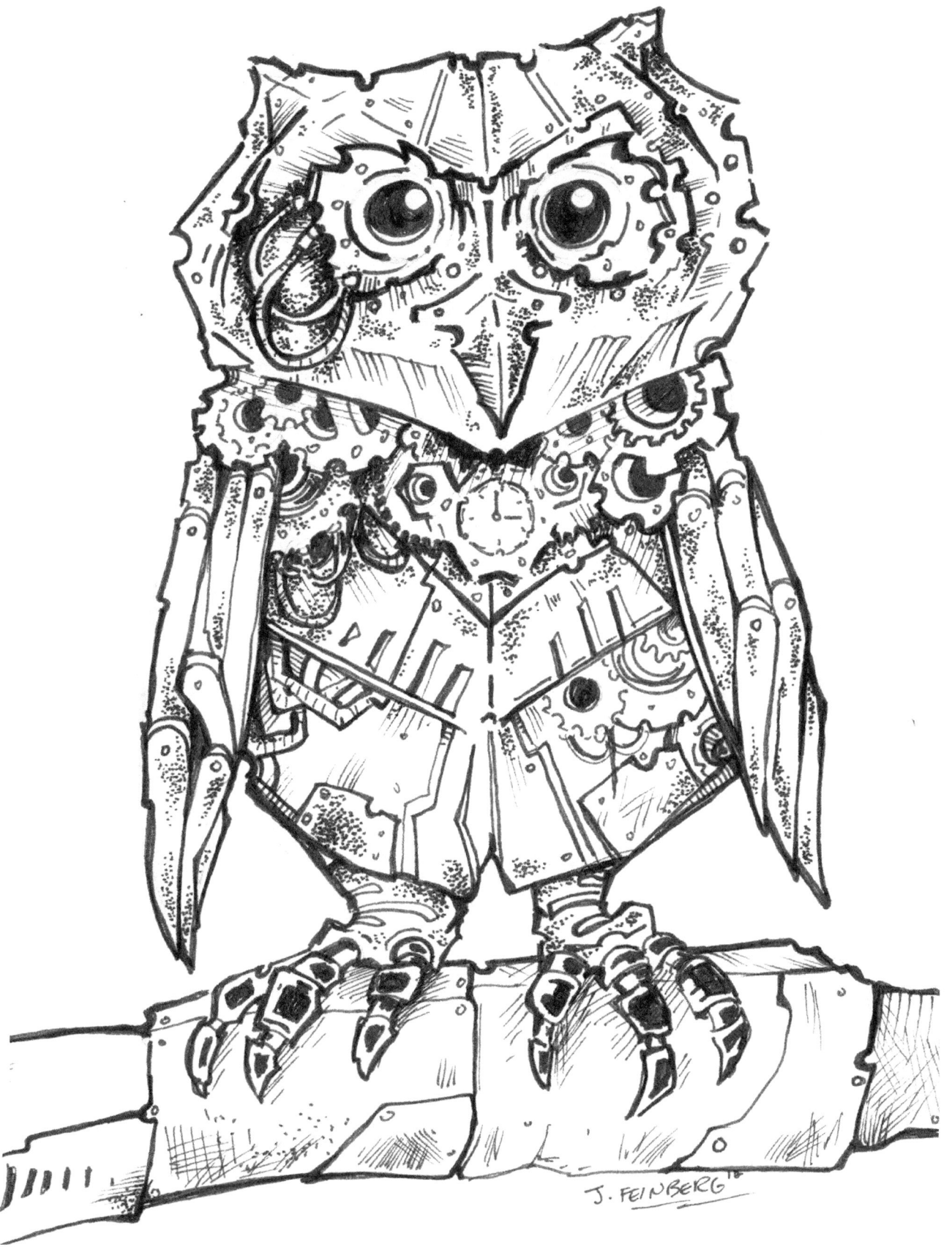

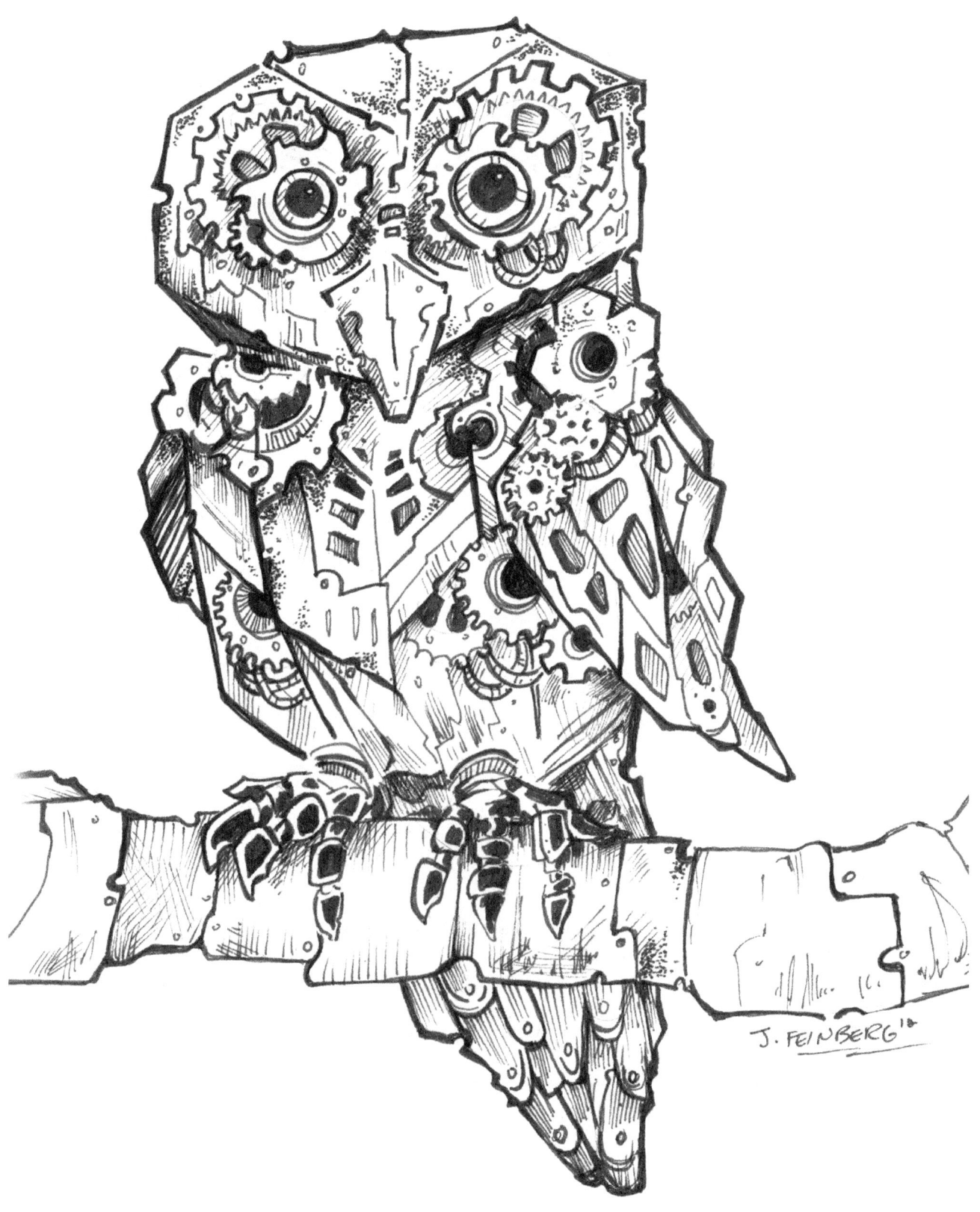

J. FEINBERG

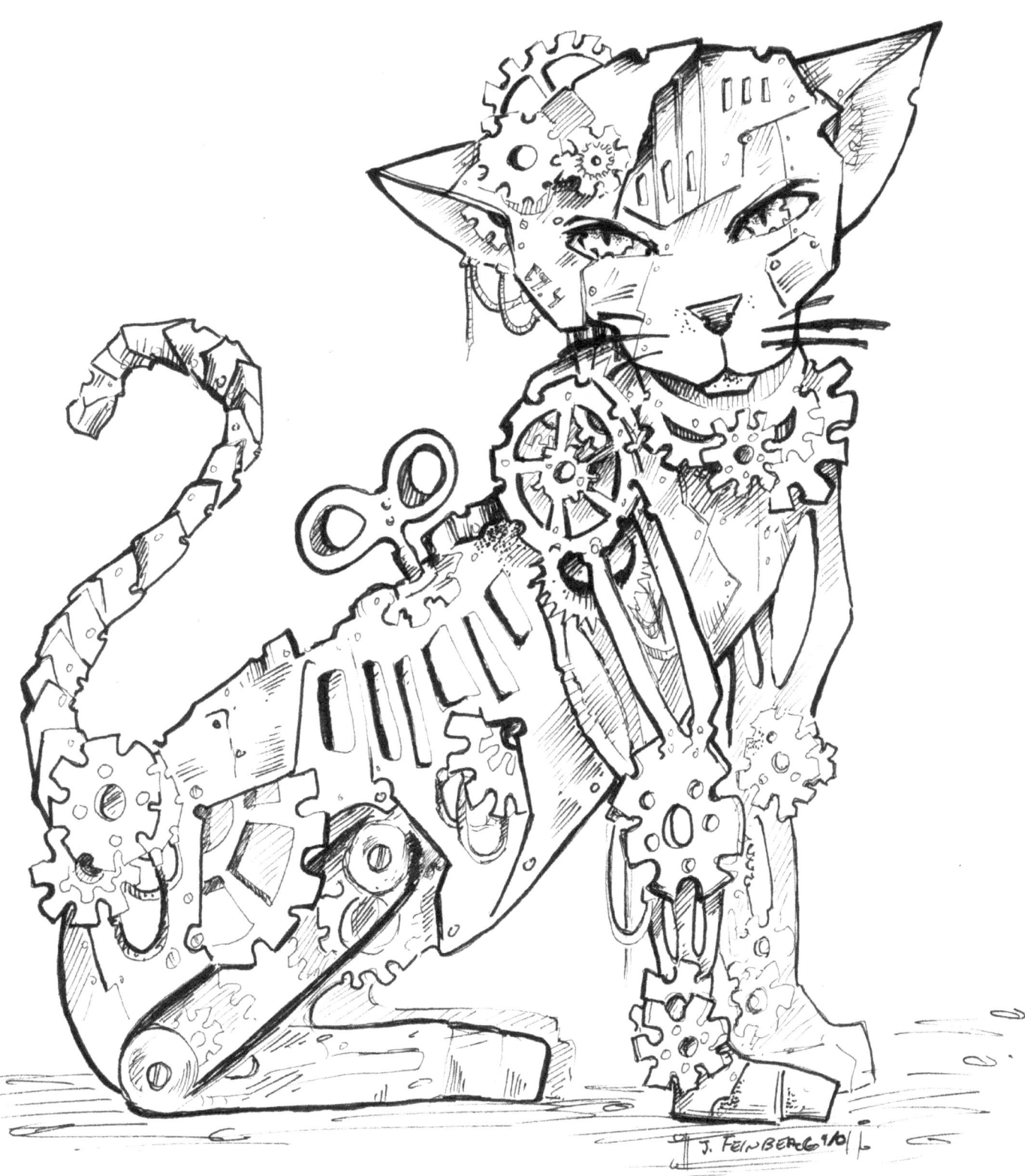

J. FEINBERG 1/0/

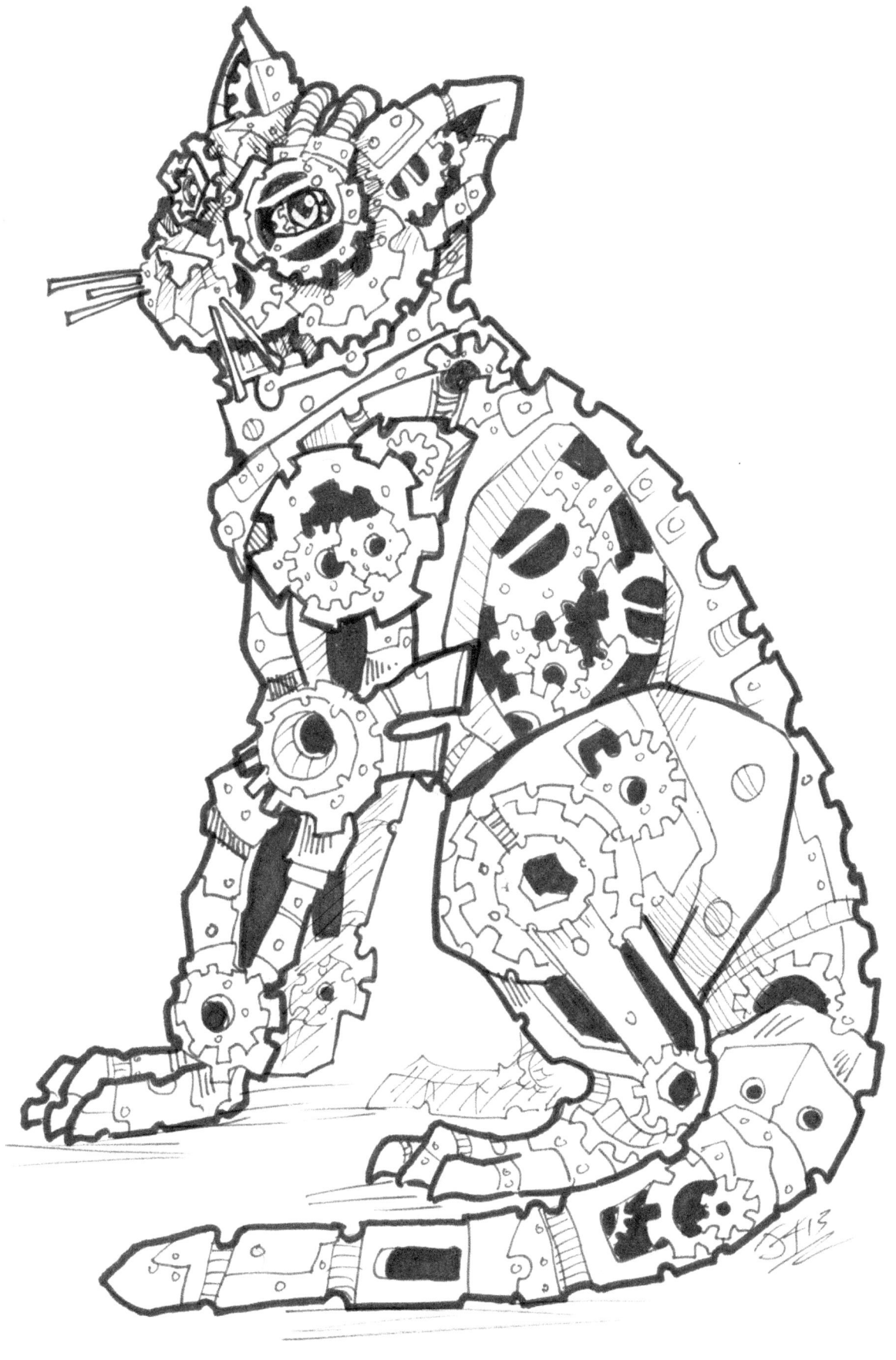

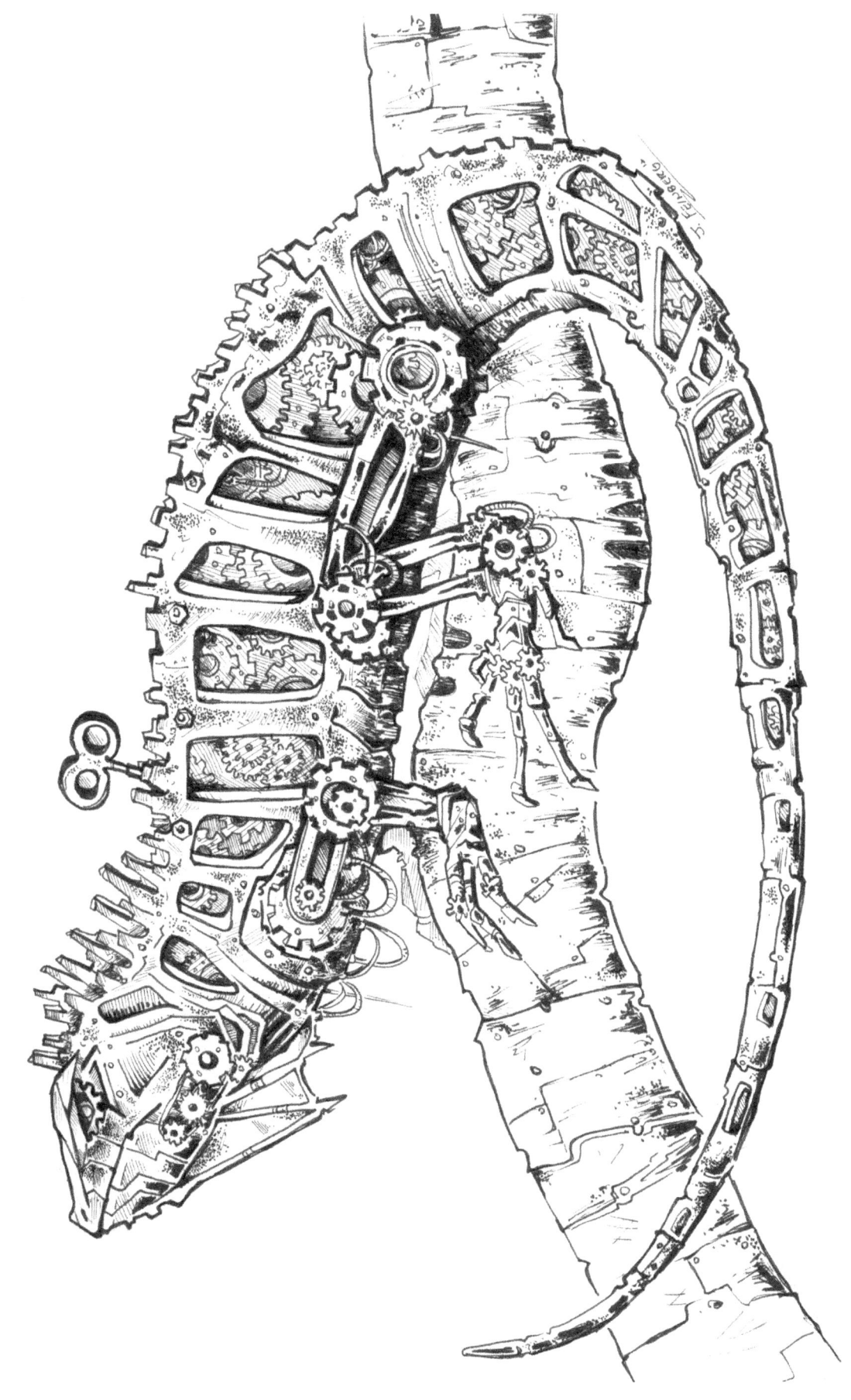

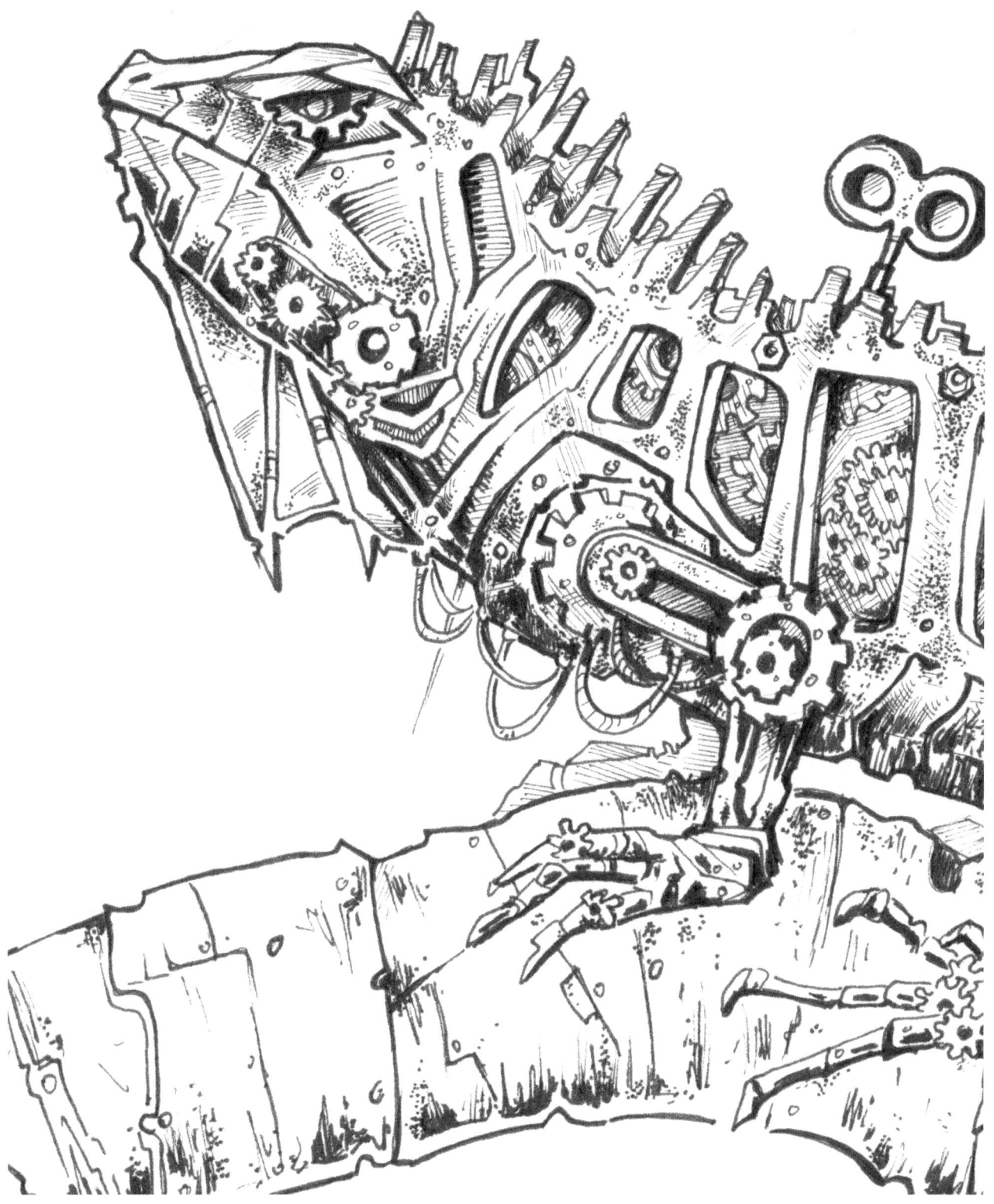

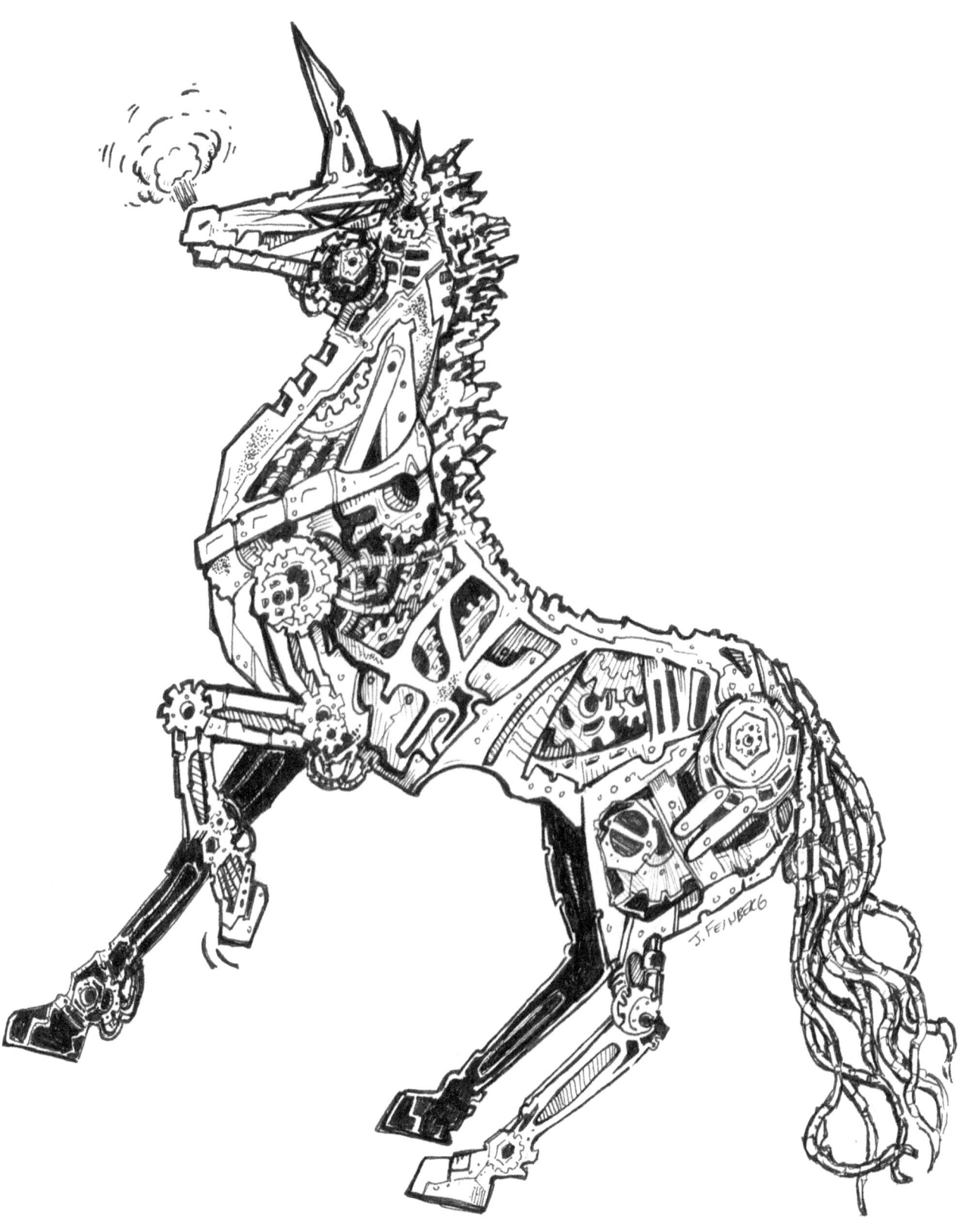

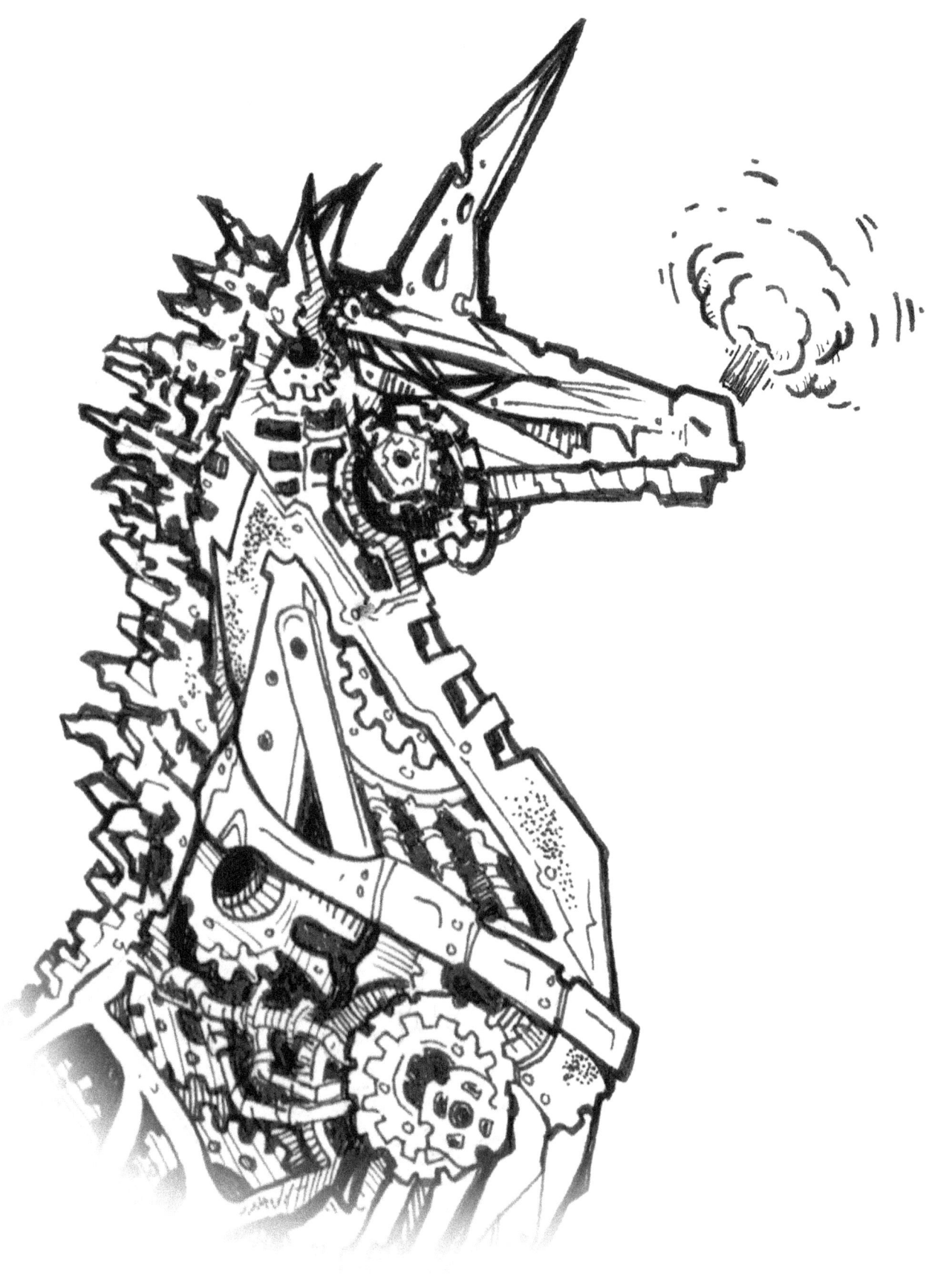

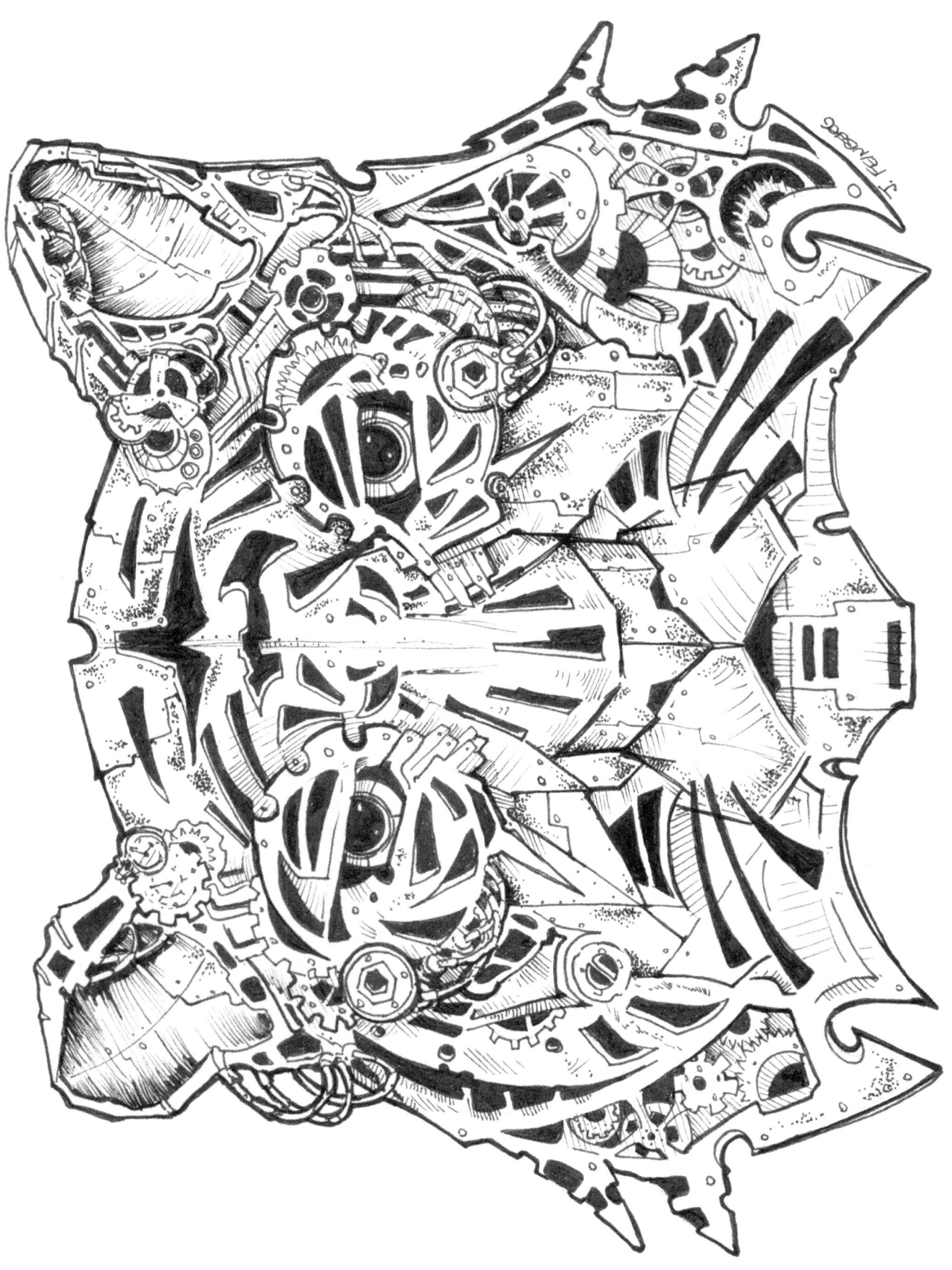

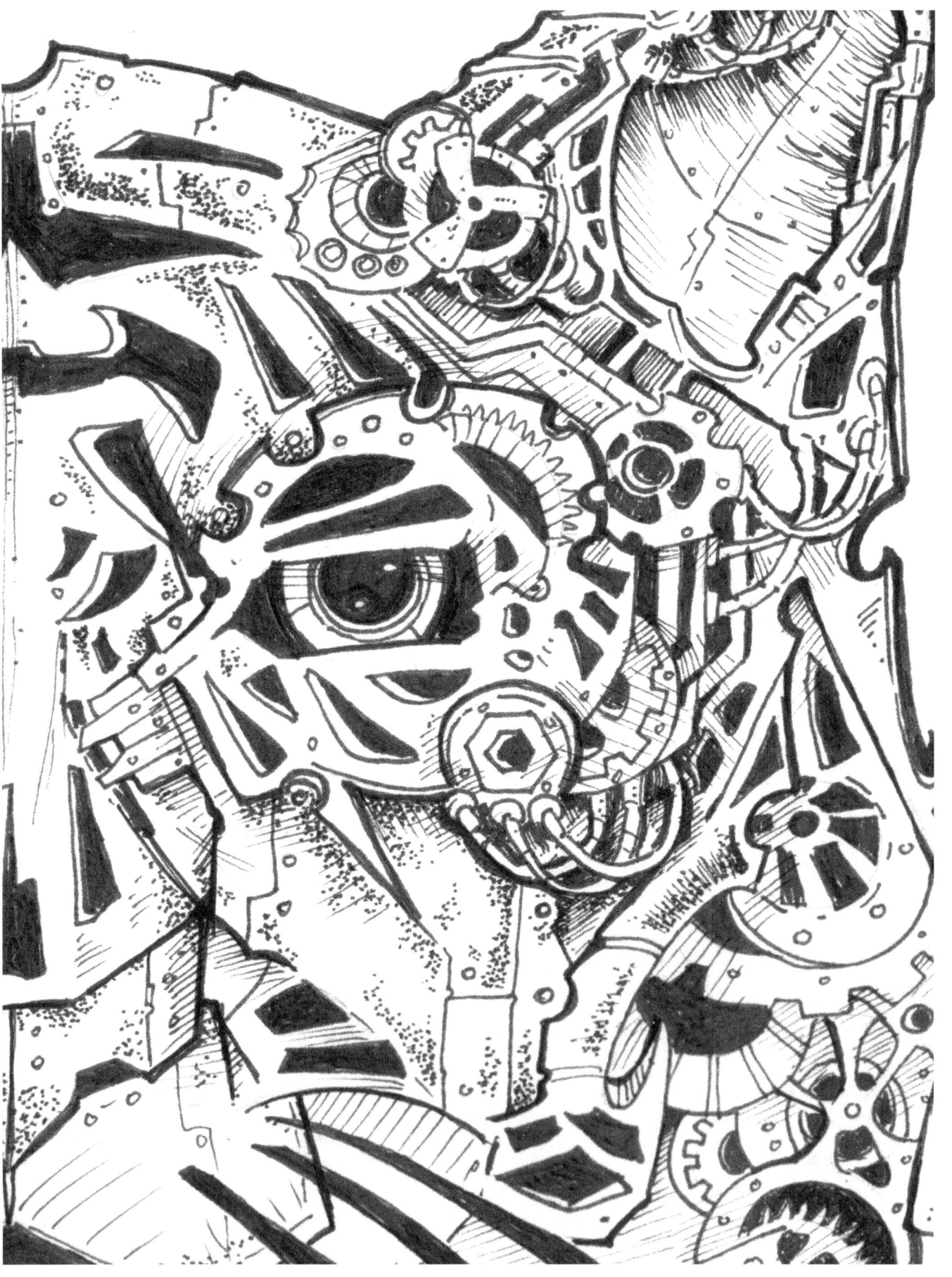

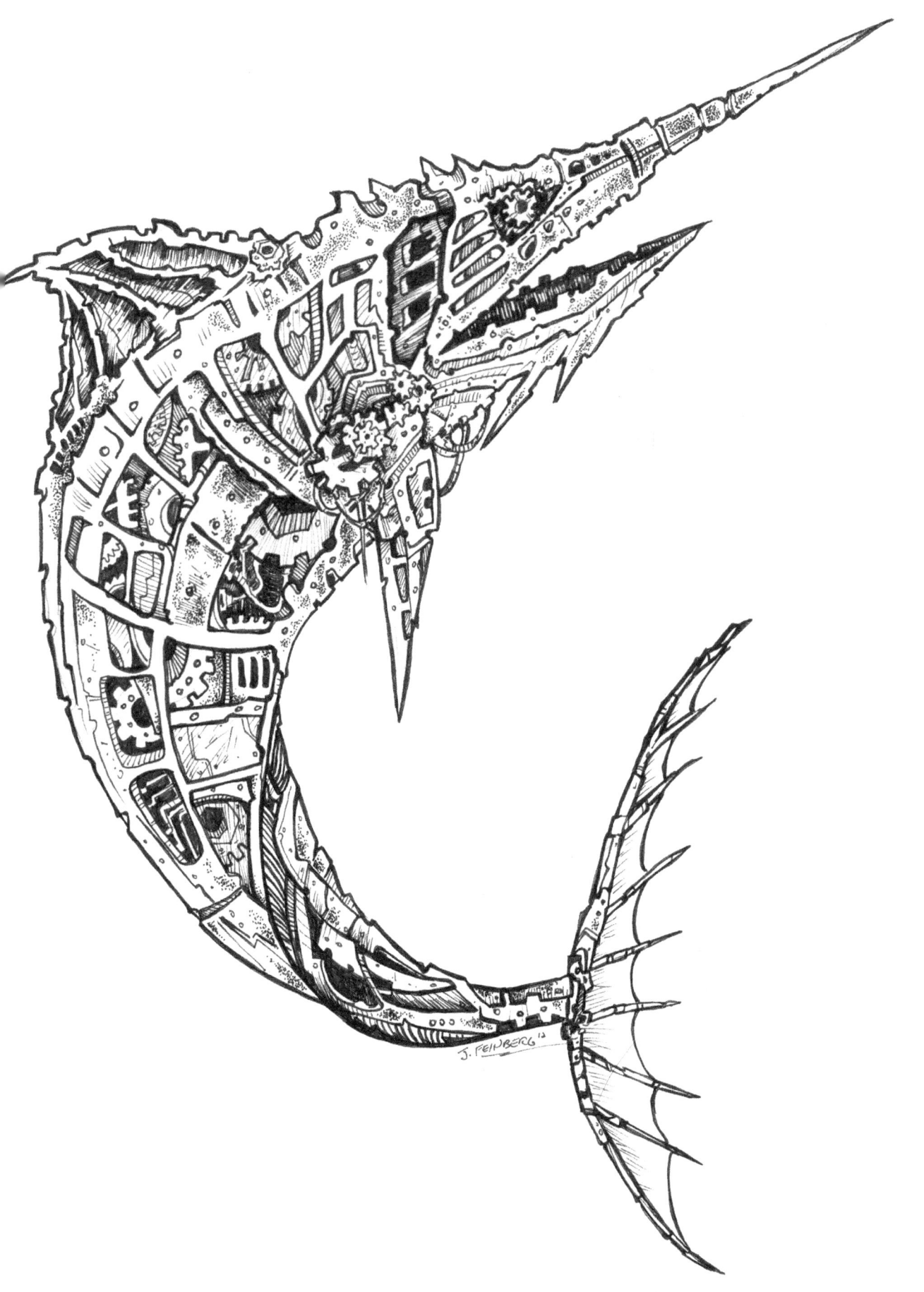

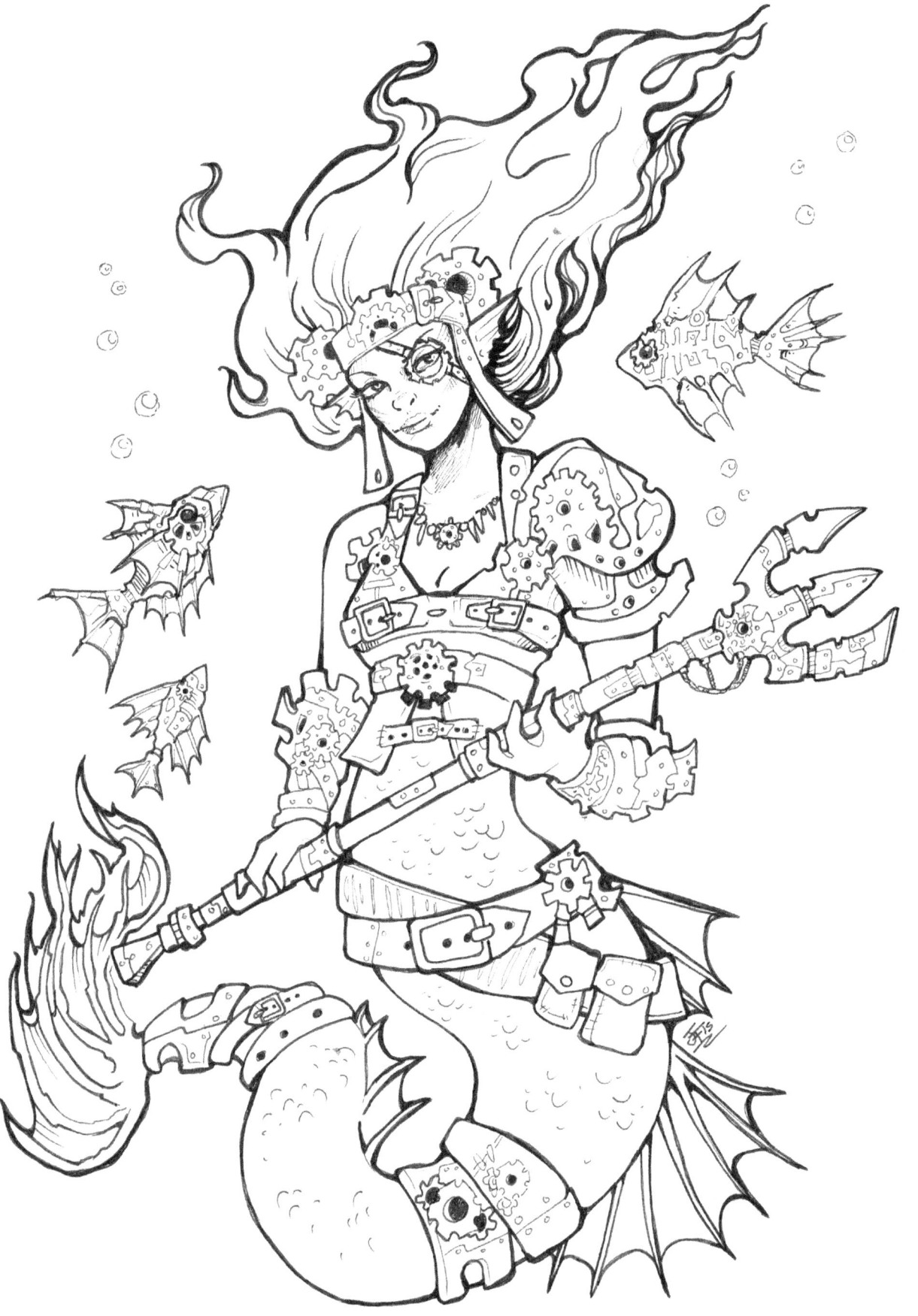

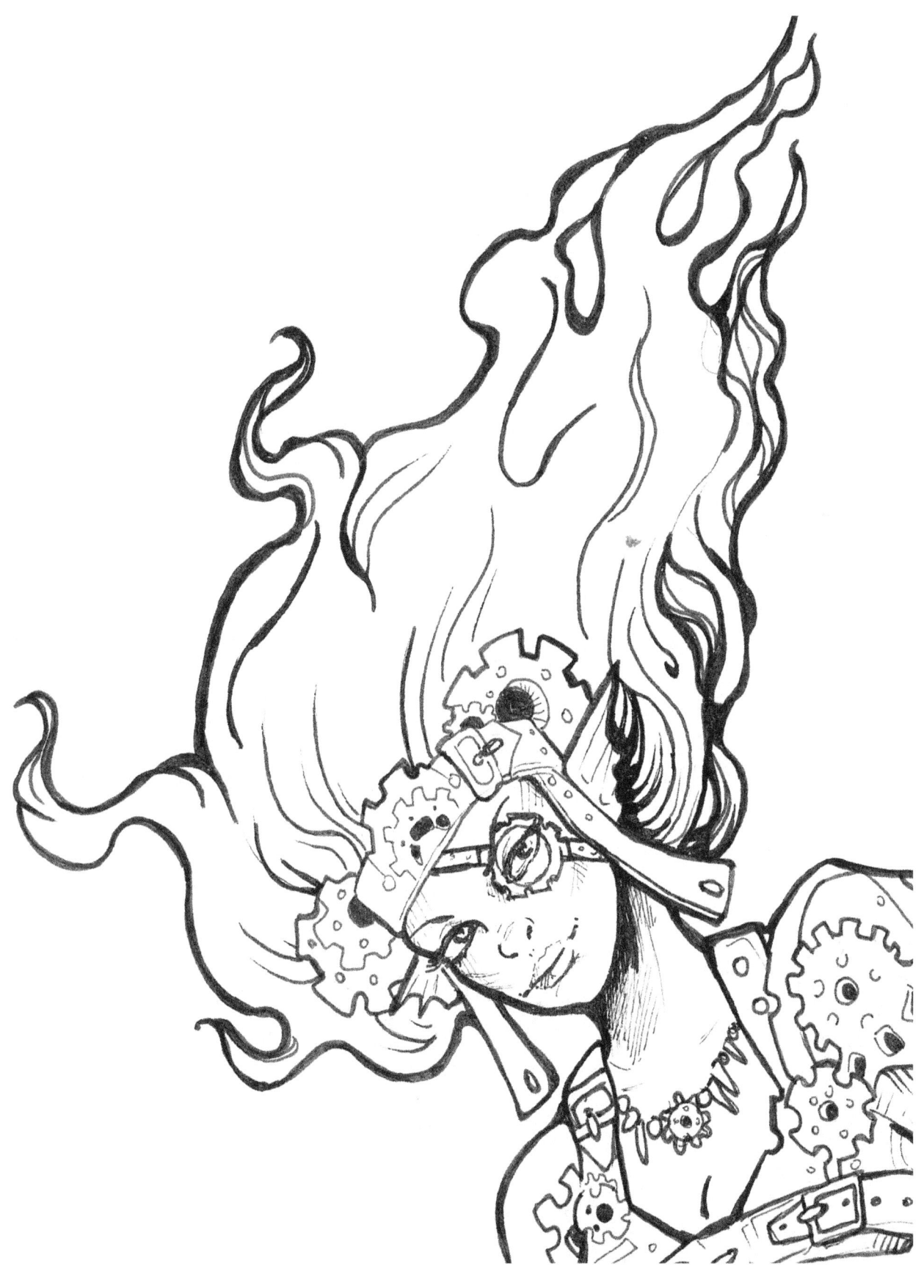

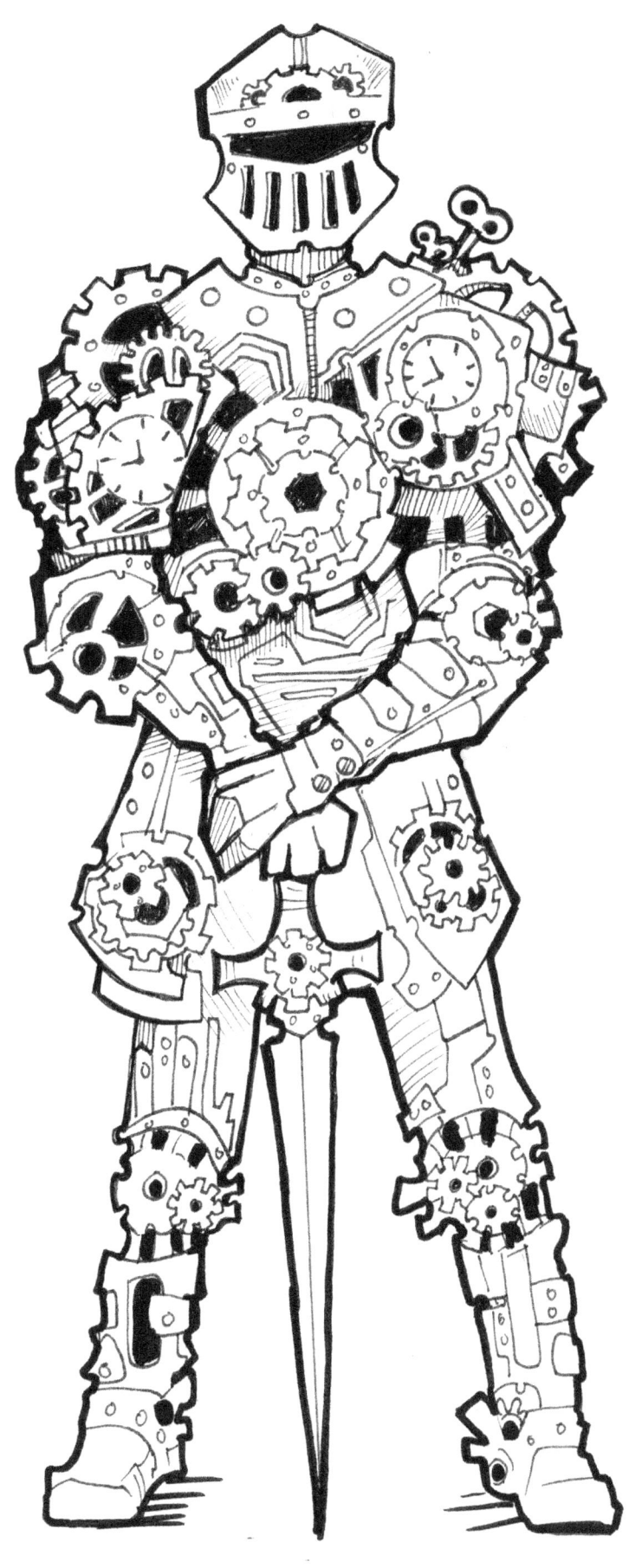

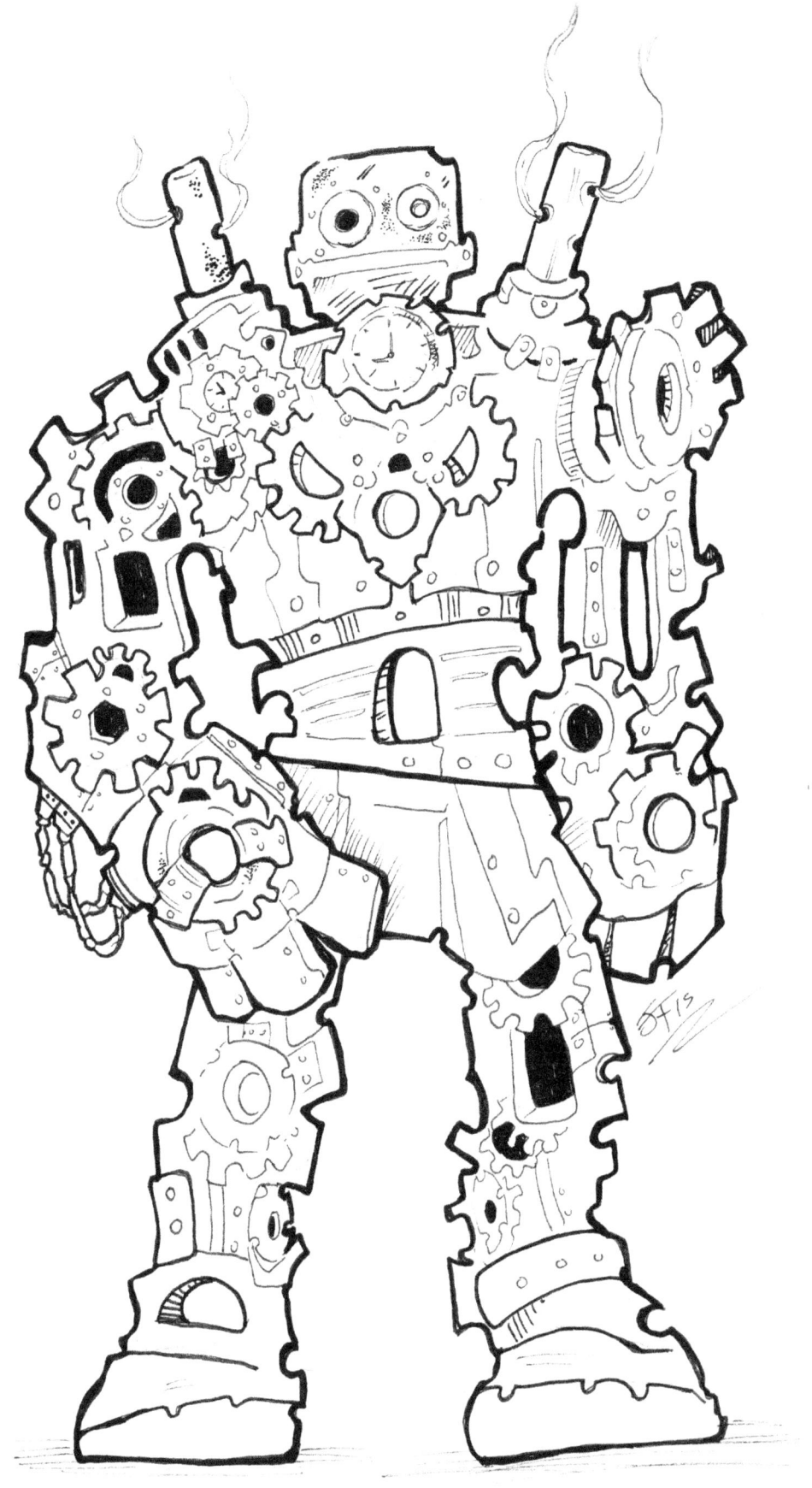

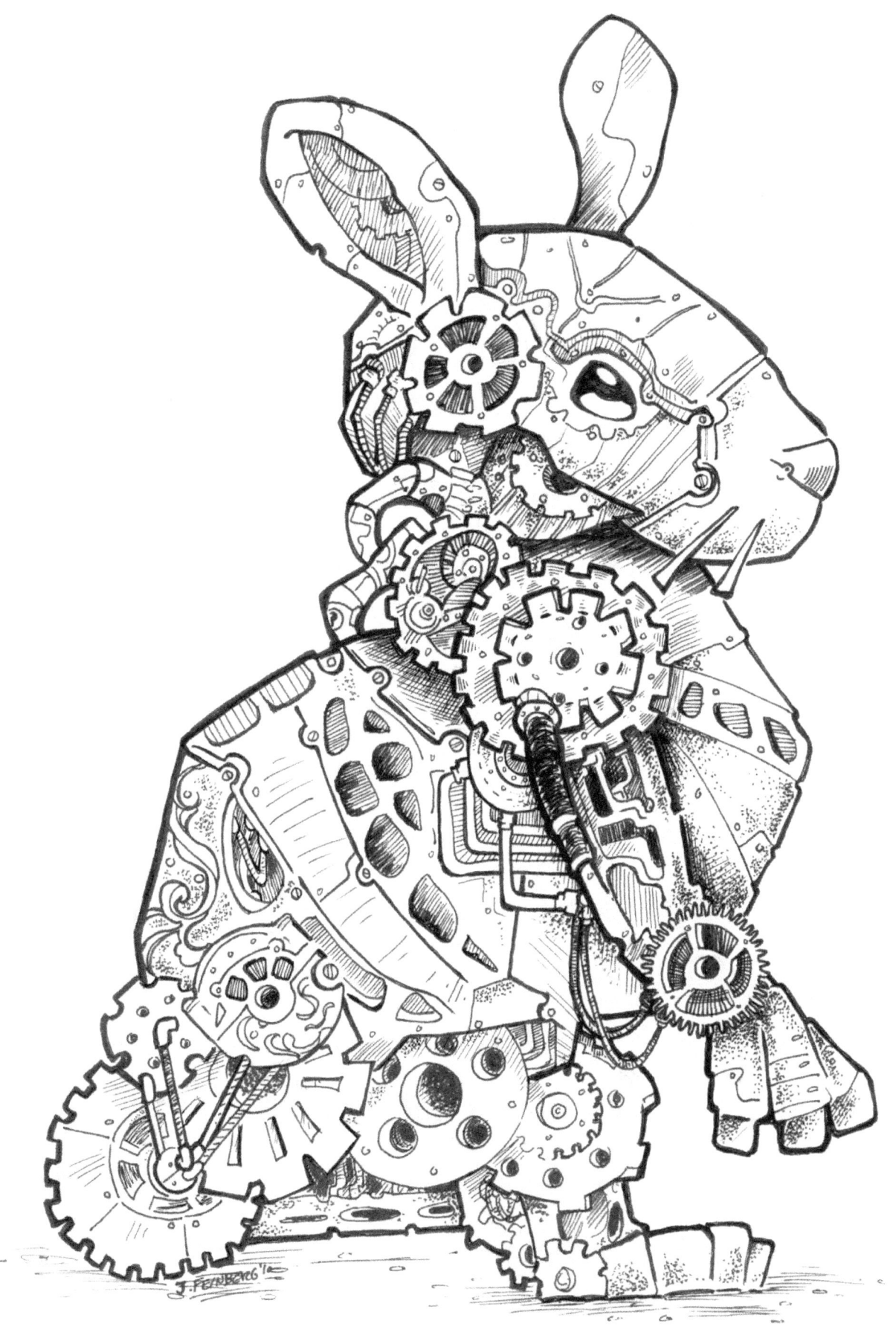

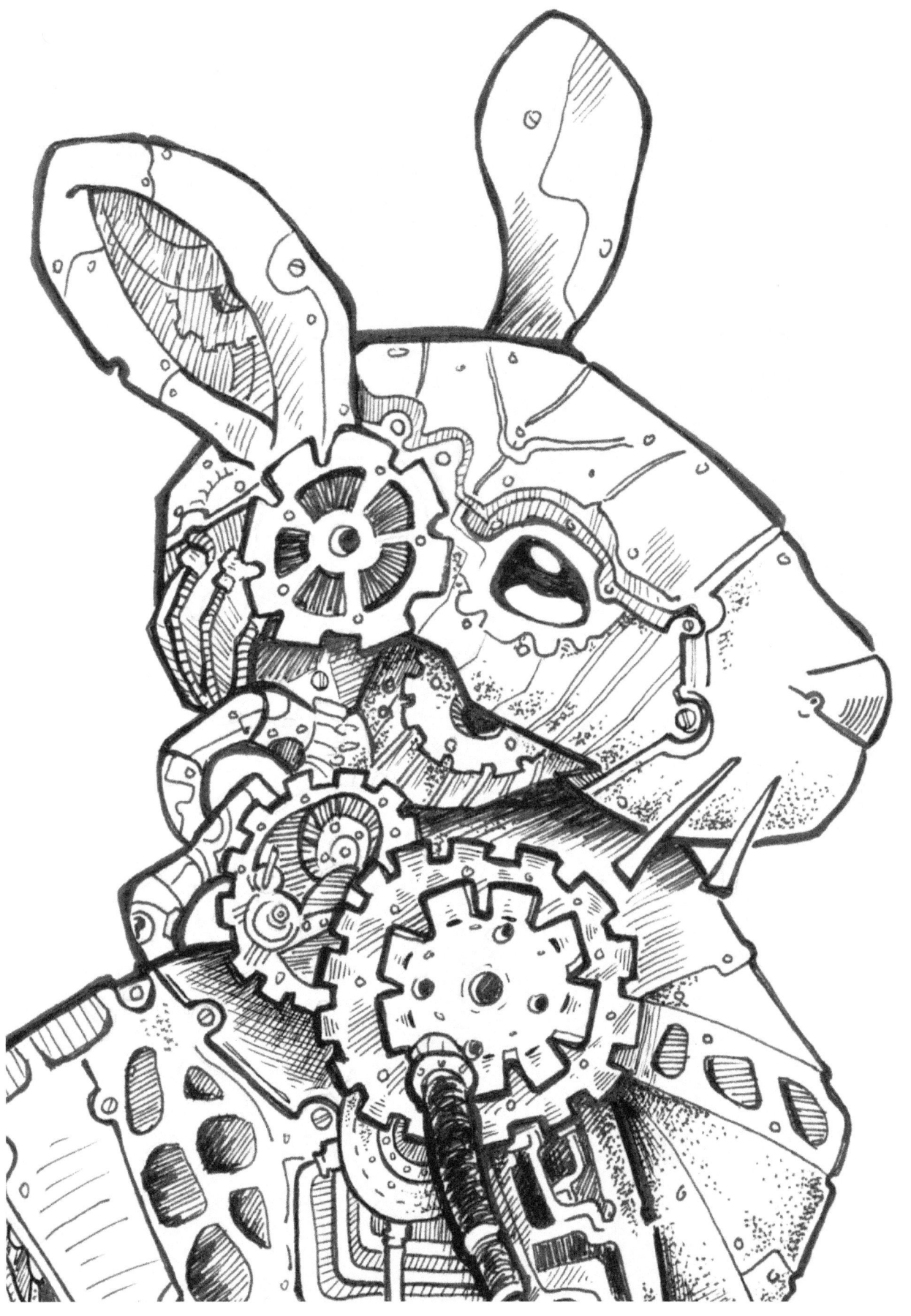

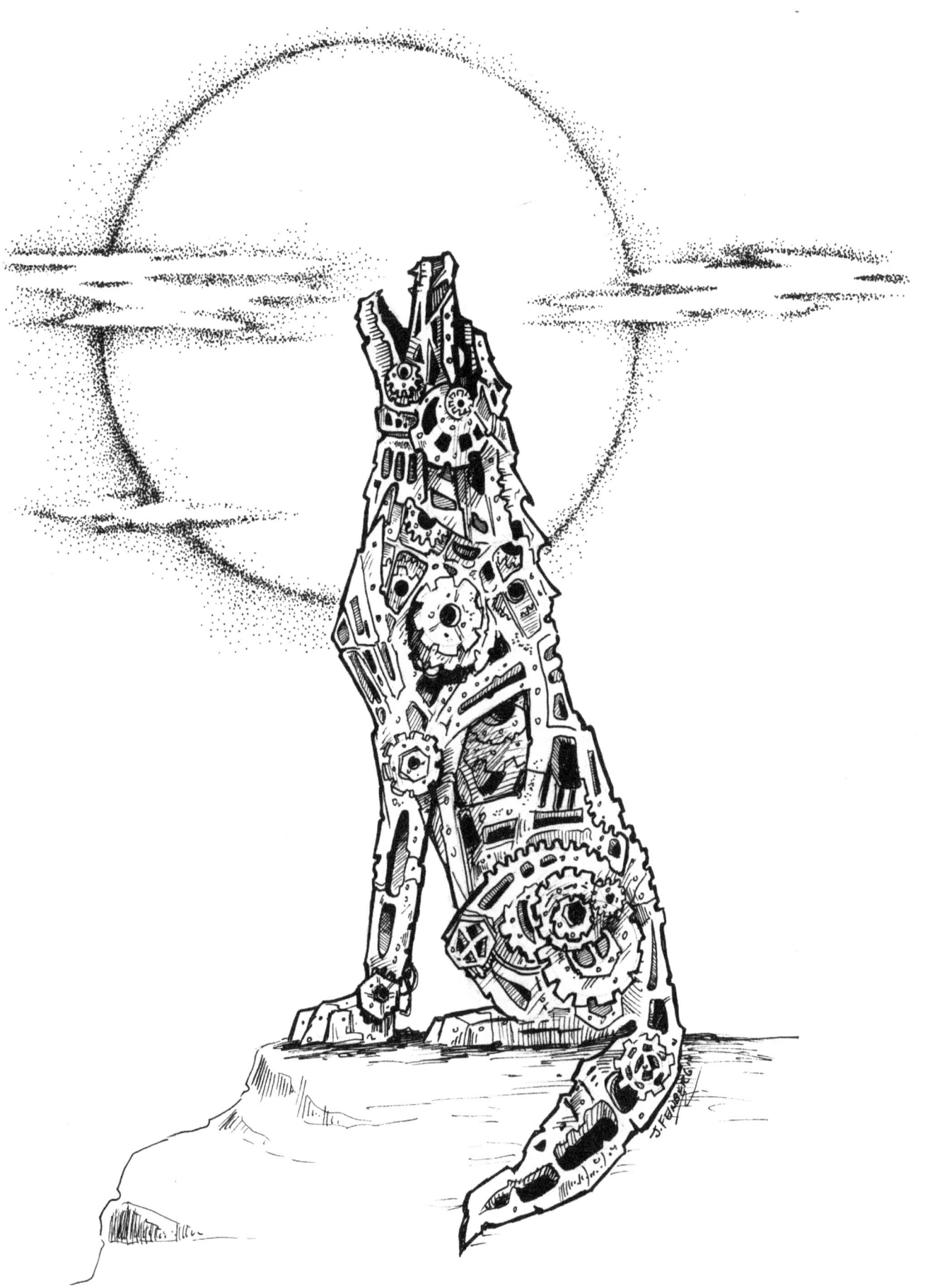

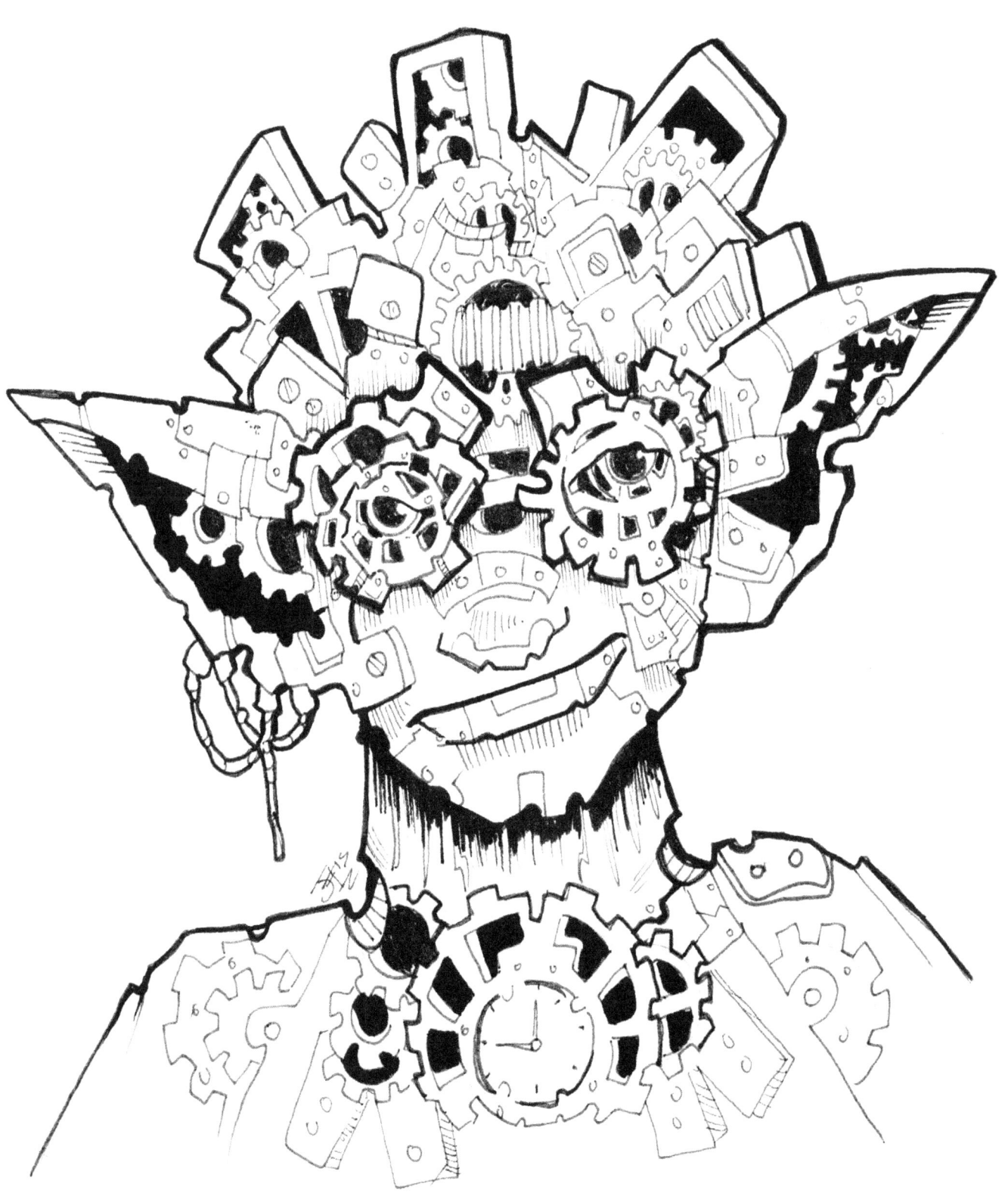

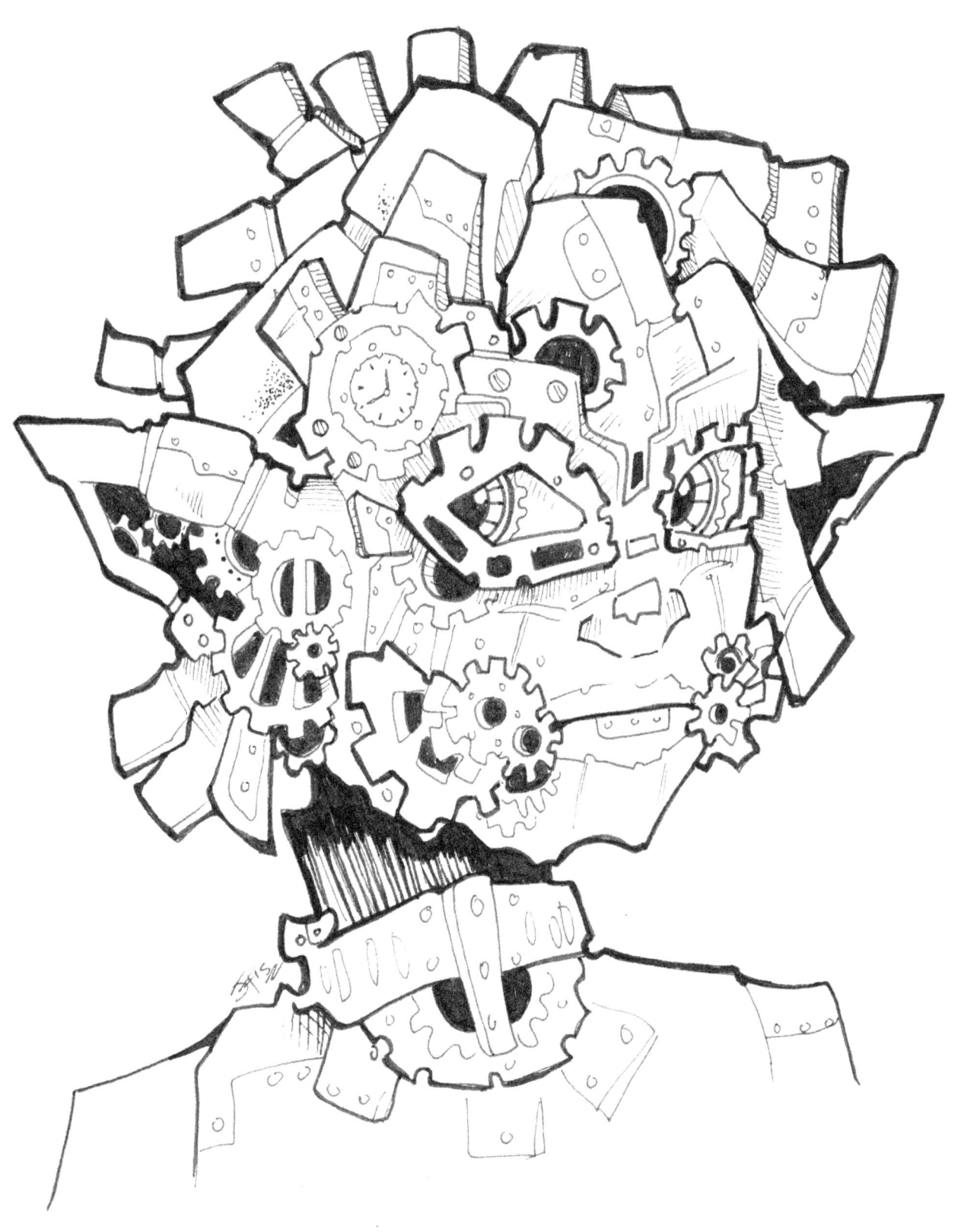

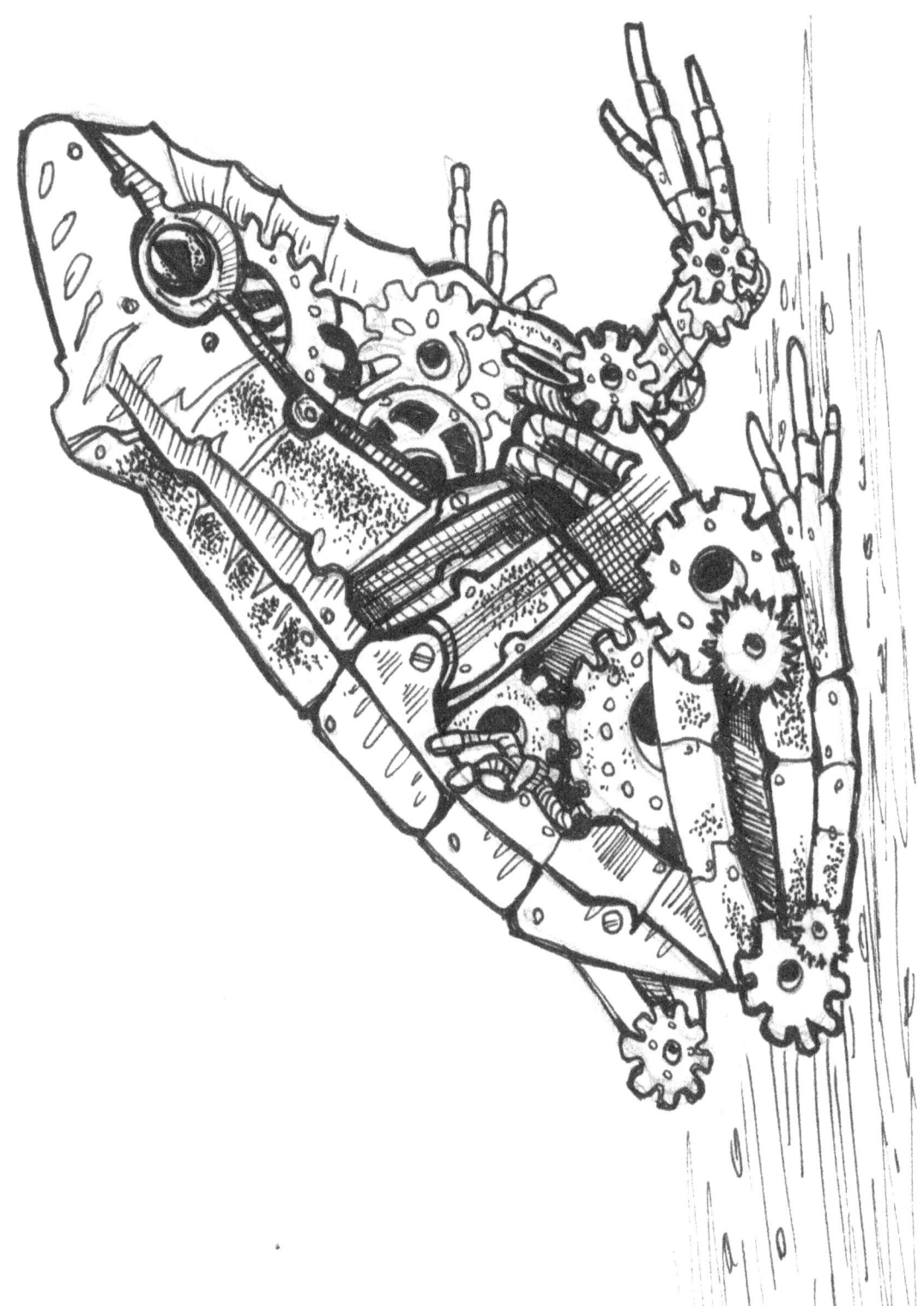

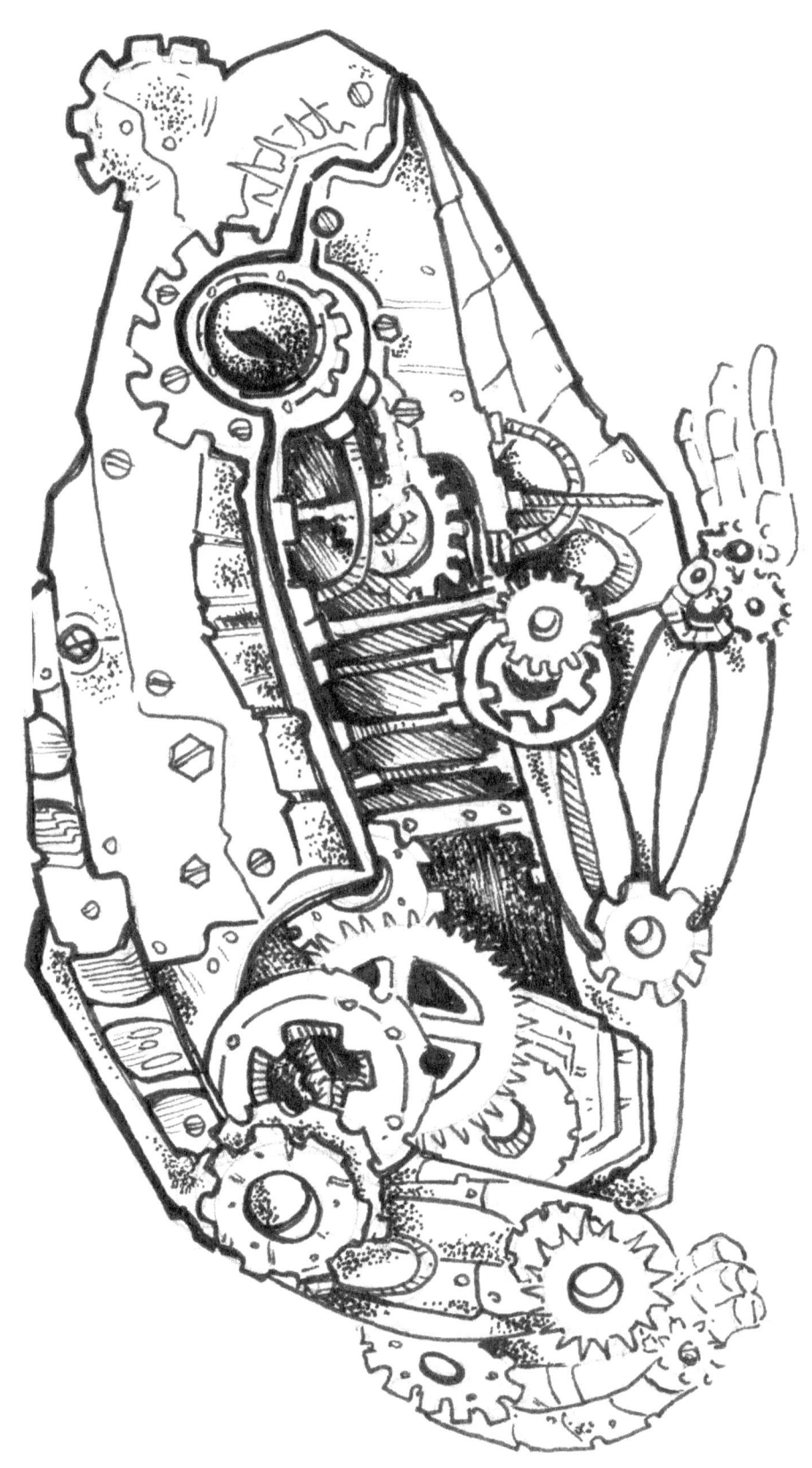

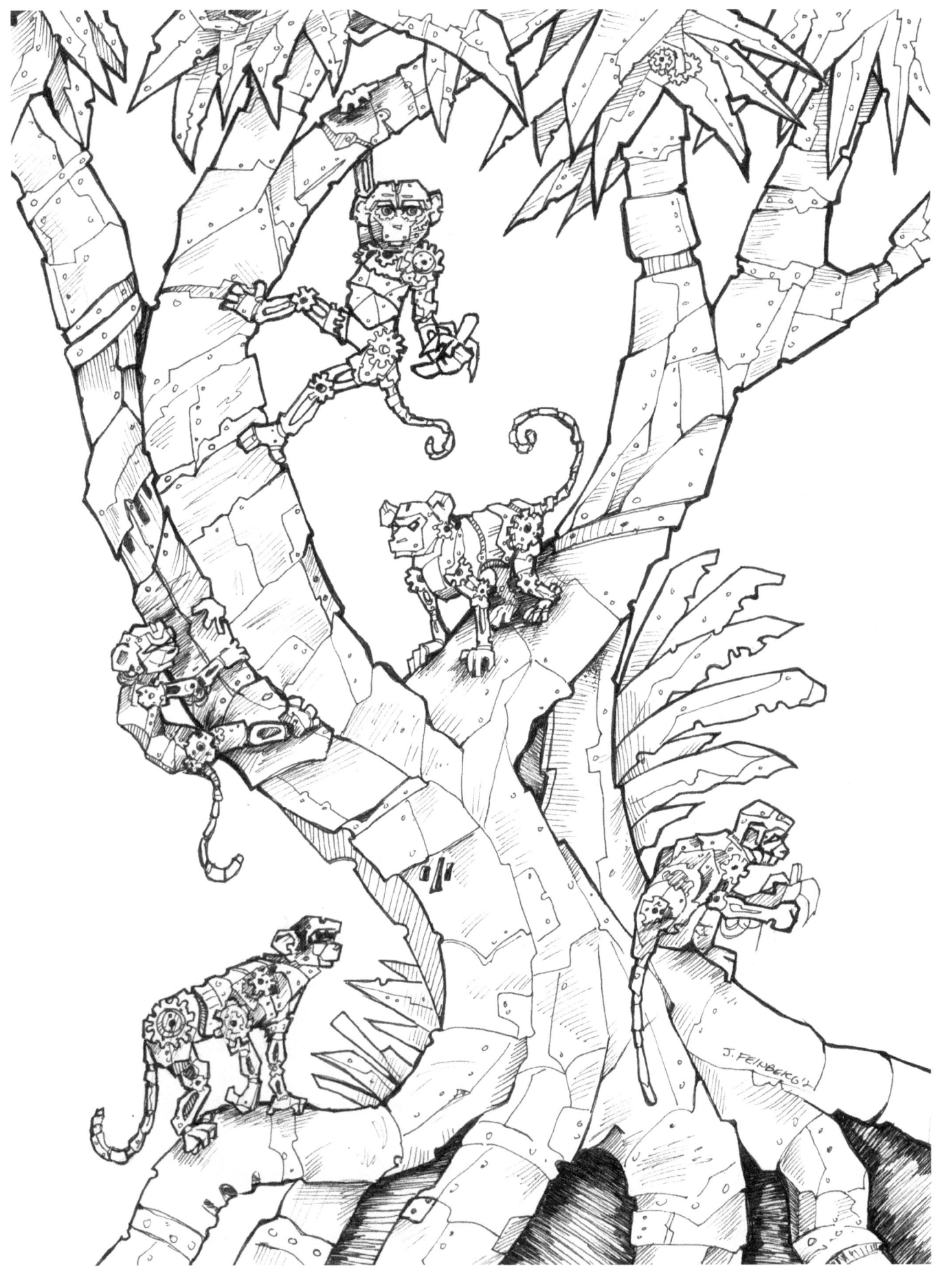

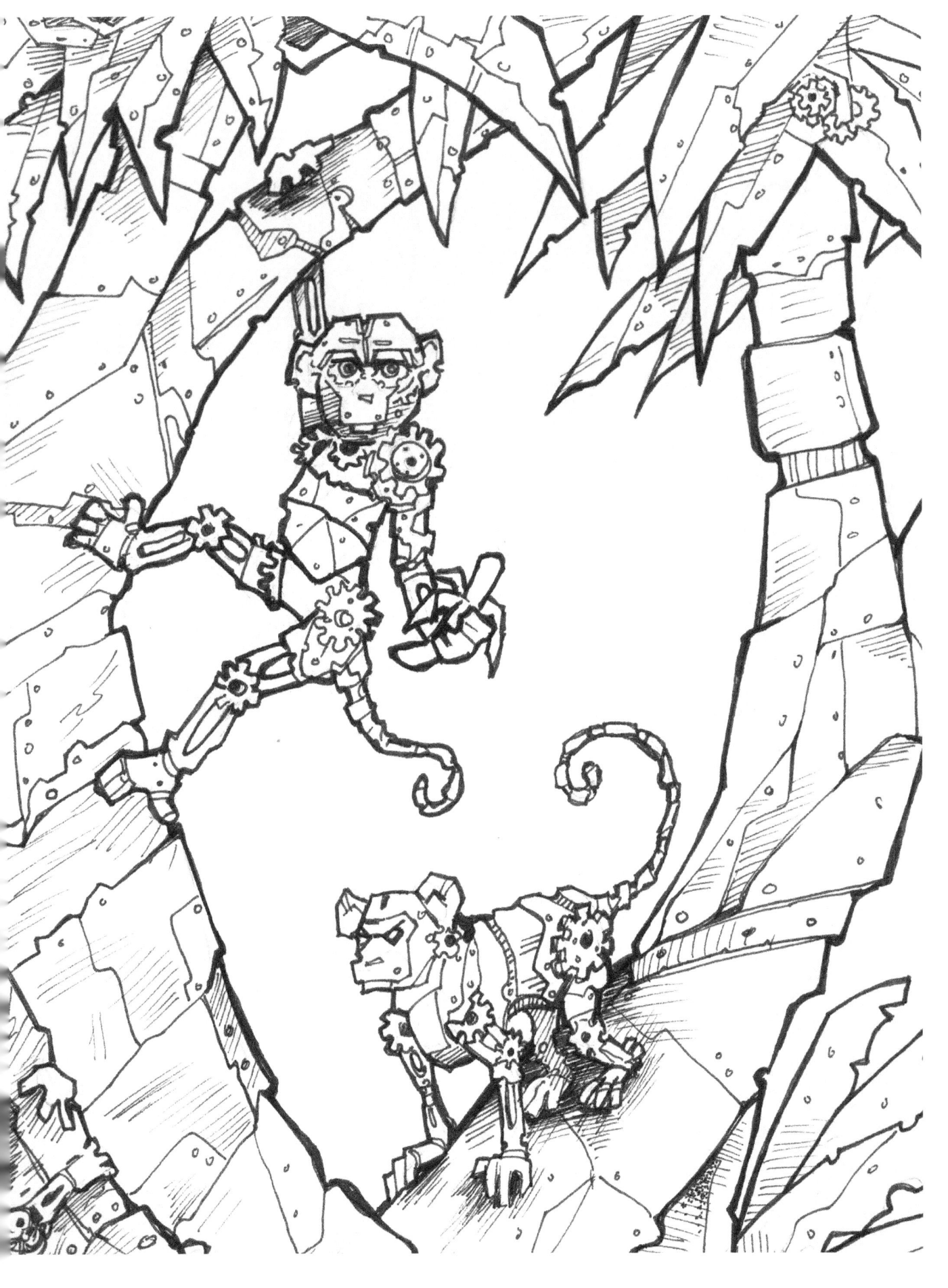

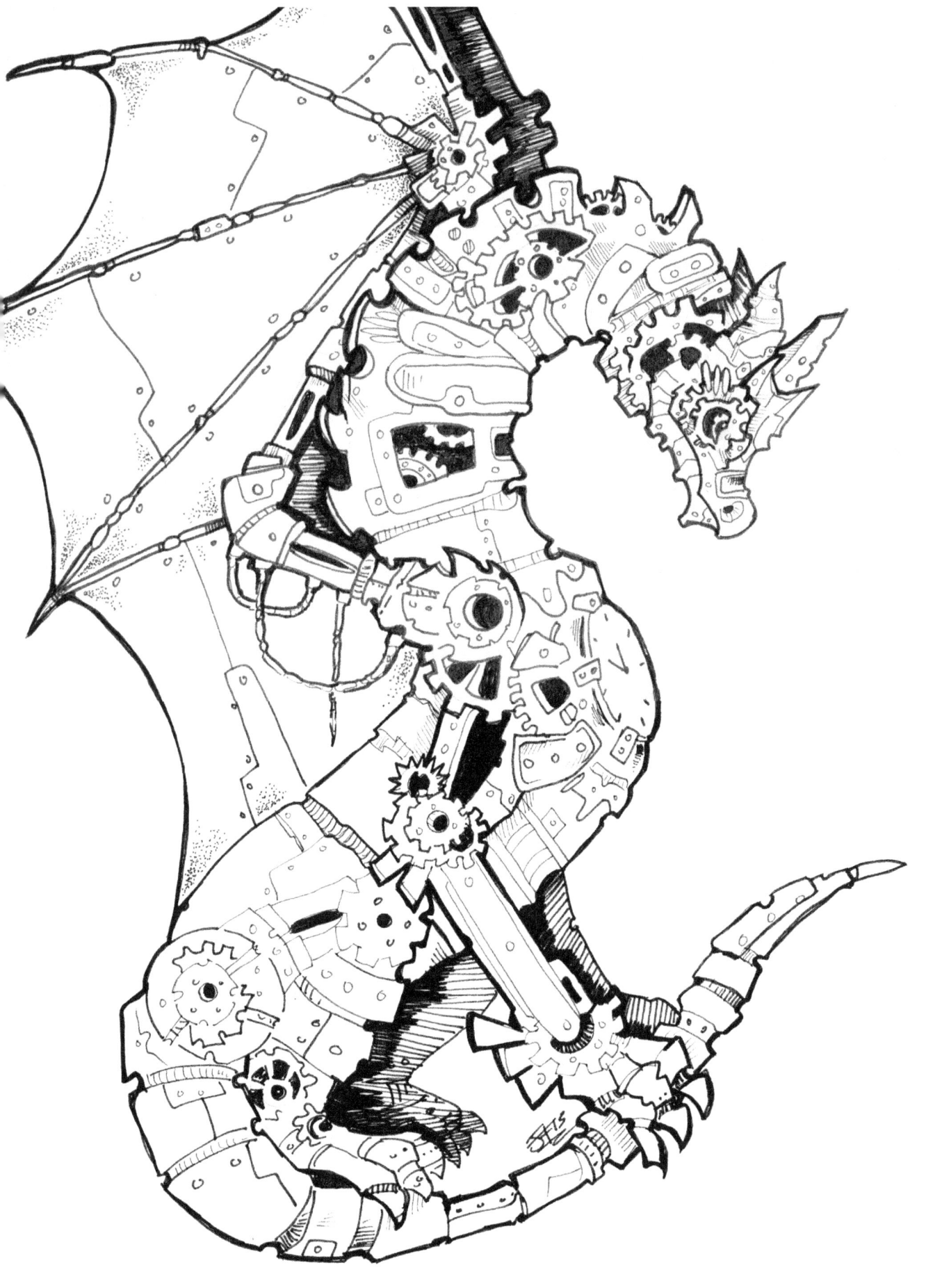

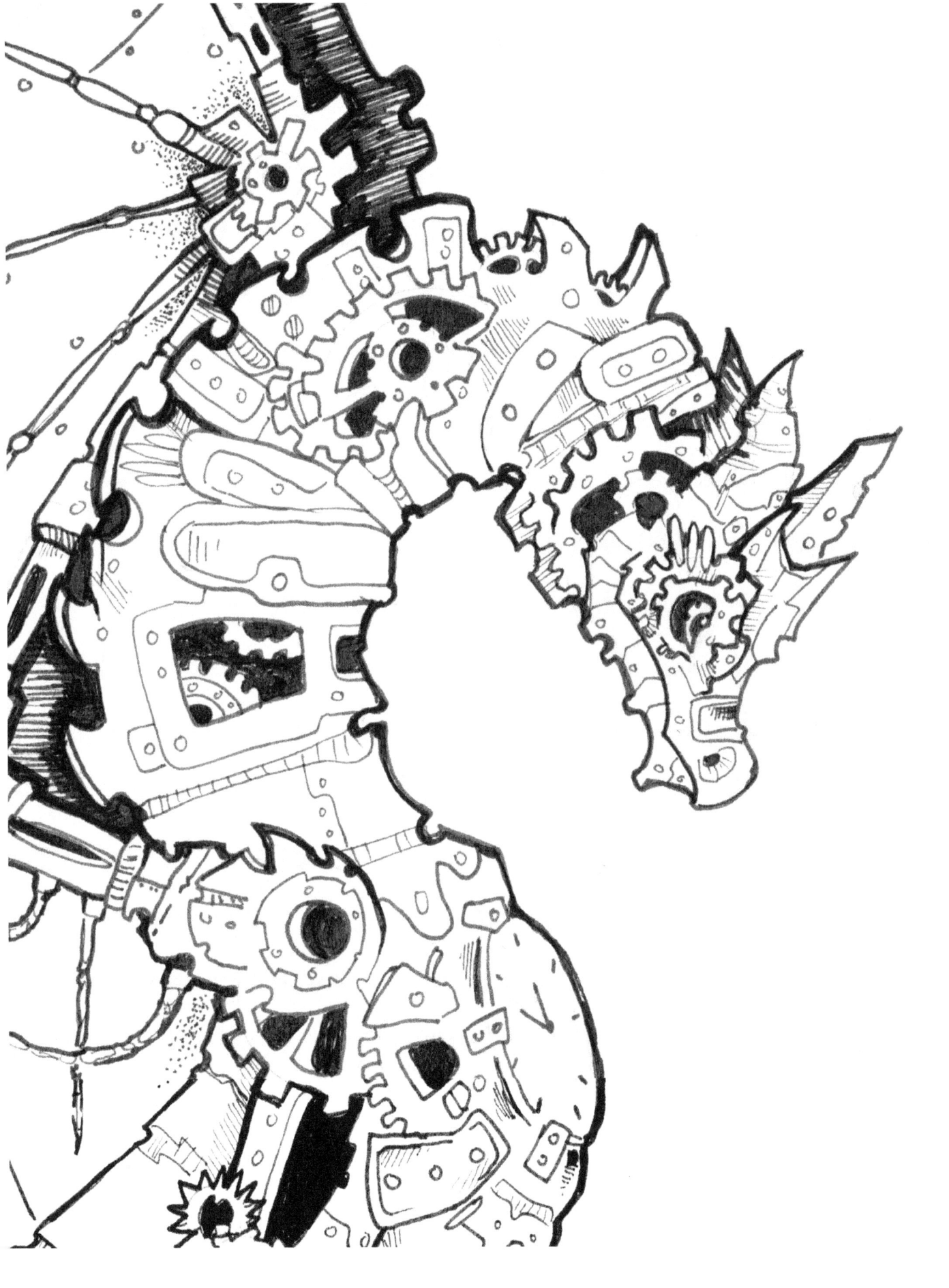

About the Artist

Jessica Cathryn Feinberg is a driven, quirky, creative gal who resides in Tucson, Arizona with a house full of books, cats, dragons, and art supplies.

Jessica has been fascinated by goblins and other fae since she was very young and has dedicated her life to writing, drawing, painting, and following in the footsteps of mysterious creatures.

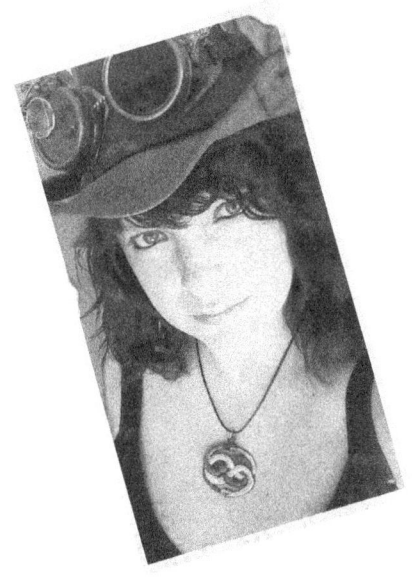

She is best known for her dragon, clockwork, and wildlife artwork as well as her field guides to rare creatures.

You can meet Jessica at many southwest events! For more information visit Artlair.com

www.ingramcontent.com/pod-product-compliance
Lightning Source LLC
Chambersburg PA
CBHW080624190526
45169CB00009B/3278